Tailwind Trading System

A Powerful New Way To Beat The Market

Table of Contents

User Agreement

Your use of or reading of this book is Your acknowledgement that You have read this User Agreement and You agree to its terms.

You acknowledge that this book, Tailwind Trading System, is for Your personal, non-commercial use.

You acknowledge that the content in this book is proprietary information that is protected by intellectual property laws, including, but not limited to, patents, copyrights, trademarks, and service marks.

You acknowledge that this book does not include reprint rights or resell rights. You acknowledge that this book may not be copied, sold, reprinted, resold, given away, traded, or distributed in any way.

We grant you a single, non-exclusive, non-transferable license for one Tailwind Trading System book.

You agree not to copy, duplicate, reproduce, distribute, redistribute, sell, resell, reprint, create derivative works of, display, rent, lease, license, sublicense, loan, trade, publish, republish, translate, transmit, transfer, broadcast, or circulate this book or any of the content in this book.

You agree not to upload, download, display, post, frame, mirror, link to, transfer, translate, broadcast, trade, or transmit this book, or any of the content in this book, to web sites, blogs, web logs, mail lists, message boards, online bulletin boards, electronic bulletin boards, news groups, file sharing networks, chat rooms, or by any other methods.

Disclaimer of Warranties

We do not guarantee the accuracy, timeliness, or completeness of any content in the material contained in this book.

We are not responsible for any errors or omissions in any content in this book.

We are not responsible for any technical or other difficulties that You might have in accessing or reading this book.

WE DO NOT MAKE ANY WARRANTIES OF ANY KIND, EITHER EXPRESS OR IMPLIED, INCLUDING, WITHOUT LIMITATION, WARRANTIES OF TITLE OR IMPLIED WARRANTIES OF MERCHANTABILITY OR FITNESS FOR A PARTICULAR PURPOSE, WITH RESPECT TO THIS BOOK, AND ANY CONTENT IN THIS BOOK. YOU EXPRESSLY AGREE THAT YOU WILL ASSUME THE ENTIRE RISK AS TO THE QUALITY AND PERFORMANCE OF THE BOOK AND THE ACCURACY OR COMPLETENESS OF ITS CONTENT.

WE SHALL NOT BE LIABLE FOR ANY DIRECT, INDIRECT, INCIDENTAL, SPECIAL OR CONSEQUENTIAL DAMAGES ARISING OUT OF THE USE OF OR INABILITY TO USE THE BOOK, EVEN IF SUCH PARTY HAS BEEN ADVISED OF THE POSSIBILITY OF SUCH DAMAGES.

Disclaimer

Your use of or reading of this book is Your acknowledgement that You have read this Disclaimer.

The content in this book is for informational purposes only.

The content in this book is provided without warranty of any kind.

We are not a stock broker or a financial advisor and We are not providing you with any investment advice.

You assume the entire risk, cost, and consequences of any investing or stock trading actions or decisions that You make.

The content in this book is derived from sources considered to be reliable, but it is not guaranteed as to its completeness or accuracy.

We assume no responsibility for the financial losses or direct, indirect, incidental, special or consequential damages resulting from reliance upon the content in this book. You release the author, publisher, and vendor of this book from liability due to the use of the content in this book.

We may trade some of the Tailwind stocks along with our customers, using the trading strategies described in this book for buying and selling the Tailwind stocks.

The performance results, performance data, and performance information in this book is based on simulated or hypothetical stock trades using the Tailwind Trading System and does not represent actual stock trades executed by Us.

Past performance can not and does not guarantee future results.

Chapter 1:   Introduction

When you read the Tailwind Trading System book and the Penny Stock Castaways book, you will notice some similarities between the two books. Some paragraphs are identical, for example, the following paragraph is in both books:

"Stock trading involves risk. Only risk capital should be used for trading stocks. It is a good idea to begin by trading on paper when you are learning a new stock trading system. Everyone's financial situation, risk tolerance, and schedule are different. By trading on paper, you can decide which of the Tailwind Trading System (Penny Stock Castaway) buying and selling strategies will best suit your needs."

There are a few more identical paragraphs in the books, for example, in reference to stock market indexes. The paragraph above and other identical paragraphs have been left intact in both books because they apply equally to both strategies. We also left them intact so the reader does not have to jump back and forth between each book and it enables each book to be a standalone strategy. Each book can be read and learned independently from the other.

We have also used a similar layout for some of the chapters in both books, for example, the chapter on finding the stocks and the chapter for testing. We kept the structure of these two chapters and other elements of the books similar because we feel that they are a very good way for the user to easily learn and use the strategies, and that is the most important matter. Our goal is to convey our strategies in such a way that the user can easily and effectively use them.

While there may be a few similarities in the writing, it is recommended that you read both books in detail because they are significantly different strategies.

We wish you the best of luck with your stock trading endeavors and we hope that you enjoy all of our stock trading books.

Chapter 2: Getting Started

The Tailwind Trading System is a unique trading system that has proven to be powerful and very profitable. It is easy to learn and can be used by beginners and experienced stock traders. You will not need any charting software or subscription services to use the Tailwind Trading System. All of the information that you need to use this stock trading system is included in this book.

Stock trading involves risk. Only risk capital should be used for trading stocks. It is a good idea to begin by trading on paper when you are learning a new stock trading system. Everyone's financial situation, risk tolerance, and schedule are different. By trading on paper, you can decide which of the Tailwind Trading System buying and selling strategies will best suit your needs.

The Tailwind Trading System should provide you with plenty of trading opportunities. The Tailwind Trading System has produced more than 600 stocks to trade over the past 9 years. You will see this when you look through the overall track records and the detailed track record in **Chapter 10: Track Records and Statistics**. All of the stocks that could be traded with the Tailwind Trading System are listed in the detailed track record, along with the dates when these stocks would have been traded. You will see that from January 2000 through December 2008, the Tailwind Trading System found stocks to trade in almost every month.

You will also notice in the overall track record that the Tailwind Trading System has performed consistently well during these years. That includes both a bear market and a bull market.

When you look through the track records and statistics in **Chapter 10: Track Records and Statistics**, you will see what the Tailwind Trading System has done over the past 9 years. Of course, past performance does not guarantee future results; however, you can imagine what the Tailwind Trading System may do for you over the next 10 years!

The Tailwind Trading System is a stock trading system that has proven itself in both good markets and bad markets and may be used for many years to come. Hopefully, you will have many years of profitable trading with the Tailwind Trading System!

Chapter 3:   Setting The Stage

The Tailwind Trading System will utilize stock market research that is both confidential and public, and will enable you to ride this Tailwind for some easy profits.

We will begin explaining the strategy by taking a look at stock market indexes. They are an important part of the Tailwind Trading System. Some of the most well known stock market indexes in the United States include the Dow Jones Industrial Average, the S&P 500 Index, the Nasdaq Composite Index, and the Russell 2000 Index. These indexes, made up of a basket of stocks, are often used to measure the performance of the stock market, and in some respects, the overall economy as well.

These indexes are used by a variety of investment products such as mutual funds, exchange traded funds, and index futures. Mutual fund managers and other institutional investors will own the stocks that are in the index that they are basing their index portfolios on. In many instances, the mutual funds and other index products are required to own these stocks. For example, an S&P 500 Index mutual fund will own the 500 stocks that comprise the S&P 500 Index and a Russell 2000 Index mutual fund will own the 2000 stocks that comprise the Russell 2000 Index.

Each of these indexes is constructed in different ways. For example, the Dow Jones Industrial Average contains 30 stocks that represent various industry groups, while the S&P 500 Index contains 500 of the largest U.S. companies.

There are also differences in how these indexes are maintained. Changes are not made to the Dow Jones Industrial Average very often. The last time a change was made to the Dow Jones Industrial Average was in 2004 when AIG, Pfizer, and Verizon were added to the index. On the other hand, the S&P 500 Index may be changed several times a year.

The Tailwind Trading System will concentrate on three stock market indexes. These three indexes are Standard and Poor's three main U.S. indexes. They are the S&P 500 Index, the S&P MidCap 400 Index, and the S&P SmallCap 600 Index.

Standard and Poor's has written a publication titled *S&P U.S. Indices Index Methodology* [1]. In this publication they state that Standard & Poor's U.S. indices are maintained by the U.S. Index Committee. They also state that there are eight members of the Committee; all are full-time professional members of Standard & Poor's staff, and the Committee meets monthly.

Also, according to this Standard and Poor's publication, one of the tasks that the Committee performs during these meetings is a review of companies that are being considered as candidates for addition to an index. They also go on to state that all Index Committee discussions are confidential.

At the beginning of this chapter, we wrote that the Tailwind Trading System will utilize stock market research that is both confidential and public. Now you have a sense of where the "confidential" part comes in. You will learn more about the confidential and public nature of this research in the next several chapters.

According to Standard and Poor's, the Index Committee also reviews corporate activities that may affect companies in the indexes, such as mergers, acquisitions, and spin-offs. If needed, the Index Committee will make changes to an index by removing stocks from the index and adding new stocks to the index to take the place of the removed stocks.

This is where the Tailwind Trading System comes in. The Tailwind Trading System is designed to profit from the stocks that are <u>added</u> to

11

Standard & Poor's three main U.S. indexes; the S&P 500 Index, the S&P MidCap 400 Index, and the S&P SmallCap 600 Index. The Tailwind Trading System will take advantage of Standard & Poor's research so you can ride the Tailwind and make money!

So, what happens to the stocks after they have been added to these indexes? Well, some may go up and some may go down. It is difficult to tell, unless you use the Tailwind Trading System and our proprietary formula. Essentially, the Tailwind Trading System could be considered a mechanical stock trading system. Follow the system guidelines and use our proprietary formula and you will have the opportunity to make profits riding the Tailwind.

Take a look at the track records in **Chapter 10: Track Records and Statistics** and you will see what is possible when you use the Tailwind Trading System and our proprietary formula. You will be hard pressed to find track records that are as impressive as the track records that the Tailwind Trading System has produced!

Read on and you will learn the system and the theory behind these Tailwind profits. You will also learn how to find and identify the Tailwind stocks, and how to trade them. In addition, you will learn what our own research has uncovered, the hidden gem that will enable you to ride the

Tailwind. This hidden gem is our proprietary formula, known as the

Tailwind Sweet Spot formula.

Chapter 4:   The Tailwind Strategy

Stocks may be removed from Standard & Poor's indexes for an assortment of reasons, including mergers, acquisitions, and bankruptcies. When a stock is removed from an S&P index, Standard & Poor's must add a stock to the index to take the place of the stock that was removed. These are the stocks that are at the center of the Tailwind Trading System. Any stocks that are <u>added</u> to the S&P 500 Index, the S&P MidCap 400 Index, or the S&P SmallCap 600 Index, are opportunities to make money with the Tailwind Trading System. These are the Tailwind stocks that you want to ride!

Let's take a closer look at these stocks and see how the Tailwind Trading System works. As you learned in the previous chapter, during the S&P Committee's monthly meeting, they will review companies that are being considered as candidates for addition to an index. How do you think they are coming up with these candidates to be added to an index? They certainly aren't throwing darts at a dart board to select stocks to add to their indexes. It's also a good bet that they are probably not picking stocks out of a hat either. No, they're doing their homework on these stocks.

In their *S&P U.S. Indices Index Methodology* [1] publication, Standard & Poor's states that there are some basic requirements that a stock must meet before it can be considered for inclusion in one of their indexes. These requirements include market capitalization, liquidity, and financial viability. So this is the basic homework they are doing to get their initial pool of candidates that they will consider for inclusion in one their indexes, no dart throwing here.

Now, keep in mind that Standard & Poor's U.S. indexes are the most recognized indexes in the world. There are trillions of dollars linked to these indexes. Standard & Poor's wants to select good stocks to add to their indexes. They are not going to throw darts at a dart board or pull names out of a hat. They are going to take their initial pool of candidates, which are those stocks that have met their basic requirements, and do their homework and research these stocks to select stocks to add to their indexes, and it's probably safe to assume that they have more research capabilities available to them than the average investor has.

However, Standard & Poor's has stated that all Index Committee discussions are confidential. Darn, if only there was a way to be in those monthly meetings. Well, you don't have to actually be in those meetings.

No, you do not have to plant a listening device in the meeting room or infiltrate the Committee as a spy. No, it's actually much easier than that.

Do you remember in the previous chapter when we stated that the Tailwind Trading System will utilize stock market research that is both confidential and public? Well, of course, now you know that the confidential research is the research that the S&P Index Committee is performing. What about the public research? Well, that is also the research that the S&P Index Committee is performing! Yes, you see, the research that the S&P Index Committee is performing is both confidential and public. Their discussions and research are confidential; however, the results of their discussions and research are very public.

This is a dichotomy that seems to be largely ignored by investors and stock traders. When Standard and Poor's adds a stock to one of their indexes, they make a public announcement detailing the change that they are going to make. They will tell you what stock they are adding to one of their indexes. The announcement is posted on their web site for everyone to see. In essence, they have just told you the results of their confidential discussions and research.

Basically, Standard & Poor's is making stock picks, and they are readily available for you. Are all of Standard & Poor's "stock picks" going to do well? No, they are not going to be right 100% of the time, no one is. What they are trying to do is select stocks that they believe will perform well over the long term. Remember, Standard & Poor's three main U.S. indexes, the S&P 500 Index, the S&P MidCap 400 Index, and the S&P SmallCap 600 Index, are used by a variety of investment products such as mutual funds, exchange traded funds, and index futures. There are trillions of dollars linked to these three indexes through these various investment products. Standard and Poor's does not want to see their indexes go down in value. They want their indexes to increase in value over the long term, so they are going to try their best to select stocks that they believe will perform well over the long term.

The Tailwind Trading System will take advantage of these S&P "stock picks" so that you can ride the Tailwind for some easy profits. Realizing that the result of Standard & Poor's research is public, and that they are trying to select good stocks, we set out to find a way to profit from this research. We also took into consideration the fact that the S&P "stock picks" are more long term in nature.

We wrote our own custom software programs to analyze the data. We ran the data forward and backward, sorted and unsorted it, categorized and subcategorized it. We ran it through many different parameters and scenarios. It took a lot of time and effort, and it paid off. We uncovered a hidden gem that we call the Tailwind Sweet Spot.

The Tailwind Sweet Spot, our proprietary formula, is a combination of an event, a specific day, and a filter. You can think of it in terms of this formula:

Tailwind Sweet Spot = Event + Day + Filter

First, we'll take a look at the Tailwind part of this formula and see where the Event comes in. When Standard & Poor's announces that they are adding a stock to one of their indexes, Wall Street takes notice. Fund managers and other institutional investors will buy the stock for their index funds. There is a renewed interest in the stock. The stock has been singled out by Standard & Poor's as being worthy to be included in an S&P index. This new found "goodwill" that the stock will enjoy, backed by the research of Standard & Poor's, is the Tailwind that you will ride. The addition of the stock to an S&P index is the Event in the Tailwind Sweet Spot formula.

Now, let's take a look at the Sweet Spot part of the Tailwind Sweet Spot formula, a specific day and a filter. When we did our research and ran the data through our software programs, one specific day kept coming to the top. In terms of total profits and consistent winners, this day was always at the top for each data run that we did. That day is day number 56. That is measured in business days, not calendar days. For the purposes of the Tailwind Trading System, a business day is a day when the stock market is open for business and stocks are traded. The days when the stock market is closed are not counted as business days, for example, weekends and some holidays.

The 56th business day <u>after the stock is added to the index</u> is the Day in the Tailwind Sweet Spot formula and it is the day when the stock will be purchased for the Tailwind Trading System. It is important to note here that the day that a stock is added to an index is commonly referred to as the effective date. So, the 56th business day <u>after the effective date</u> is Day 56 for the Tailwind Trading System.

The Sweet Spot also includes a filter. There are two filters that can be used, Filter A or Filter B. Filter A is the main filter that is used. To generate fewer stocks to trade, Filter B can be used in place of Filter A. Filter A or

Filter B is the Filter in the Tailwind Sweet Spot formula. They are as follows:

Filter A: the opening price of the stock on Day 56 <u>can not</u> be more than 4% above the closing price of the stock on the effective date.

Filter B: the opening price of the stock on Day 56 <u>must be</u> below the closing price of the stock on the effective date.

So, there you have it, our Tailwind Sweet Spot formula. To review, our proprietary formula is:

Tailwind Sweet Spot = Event + Day + Filter.

Event = stock added to an S&P index.

Day = Day 56.

Filter = Filter A or Filter B.

You will learn more of the details about how to trade the stocks with this system, and how to use the Tailwind Sweet Spot, in **Chapter 7: Trading The Tailwind Stocks**. Let's take a look at why the Tailwind Sweet Spot works.

As mentioned earlier in this chapter, when a stock is added to an S&P index, Wall Street takes notice. The stock may trade higher for a while, and then over time, it will settle back down. There are approximately 20 business days in a month, so Day 56 is a little less than 3 months after the effective date. That is plenty of time for the stock to take a breather and come down, while Wall Street loses interest.

The next catalyst for the stock moving higher will be the reasons Standard & Poor's selected the stock for their index. They are expecting the stock to perform well over the longer term. They may have forecast good earnings for the company in the coming quarters, or an increase in the demand for the company's products or services, or perhaps a favorable economic cycle for that industry. Buying the stock on Day 56 positions you to capture some of the coming upside in the stock, as long as the stock price can pass through Filter A or Filter B.

The Filters are the final piece of the puzzle. Using Filter A, the opening price of the stock on Day 56 <u>can not</u> be more than 4% above the closing price of the stock on the effective date. This helps to ensure that the stock price has settled down from the Tailwind Event. If the opening price of the stock on Day 56 is 5% higher, or more, than the closing price of the stock on the effective date, then the stock price has probably already had its run and there isn't much upside left in the stock price. Filter B accomplishes the same task as Filter A.

Let's take a look at some of the stock charts of these Tailwind stocks to illustrate the theory. The examples include stocks from 2000 through 2008. At the top of each stock chart is the ticker symbol of the stock and the buy date for the stock, which is the 56th business day after the effective date. The arrow on the stock chart is pointing to that day, Day 56. The stock would be purchased on that day. You can see how the stock performed after that day. The details about each of the Tailwind stocks shown here can be found in the detailed track record in **Chapter 10: Track Records and Statistics**.

NTRI   7/3/08   FRT   3/13/08

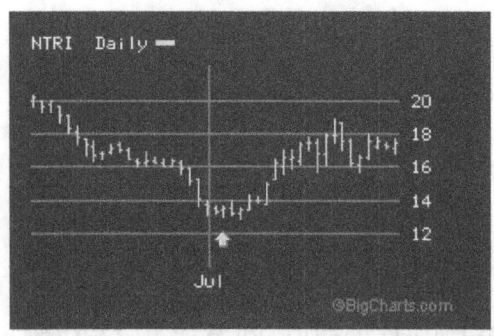
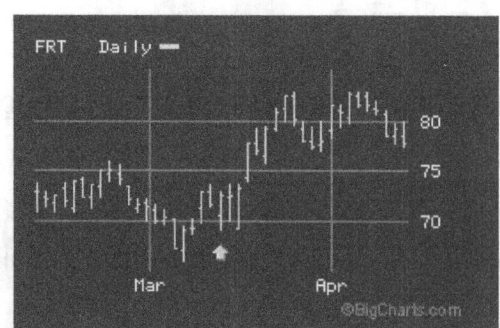

CBSH   8/25/08

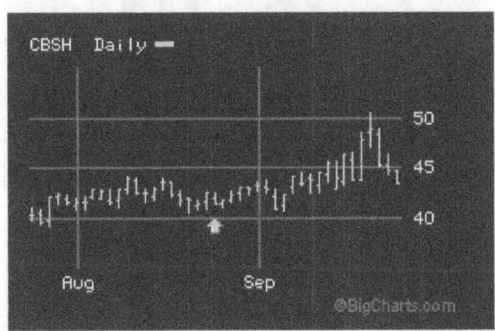

MCHP   11/27/07

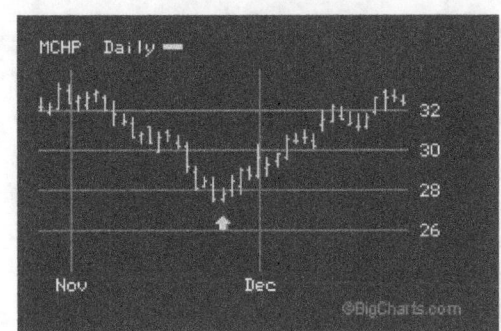

TWGP   9/13/07

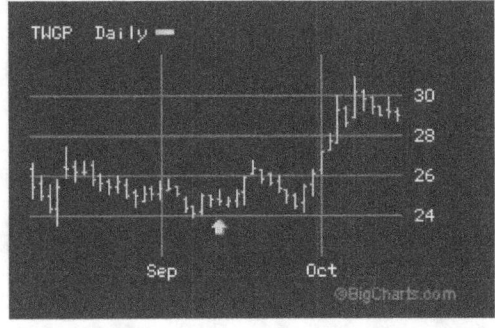

AKAM   9/28/07

RCRC   9/19/06

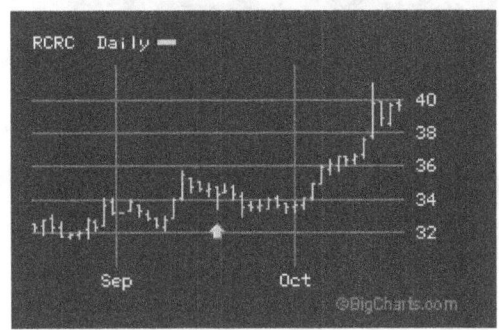

DECK   7/20/06

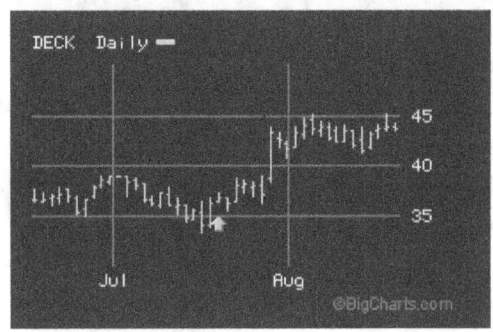

23

STR   2/23/07

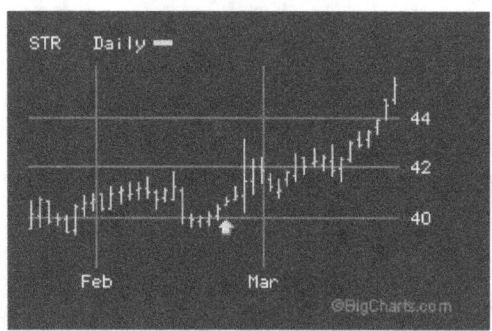

STRA   1/24/07

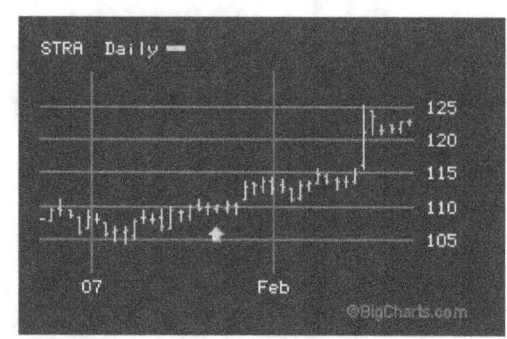

FIS   2/2/07

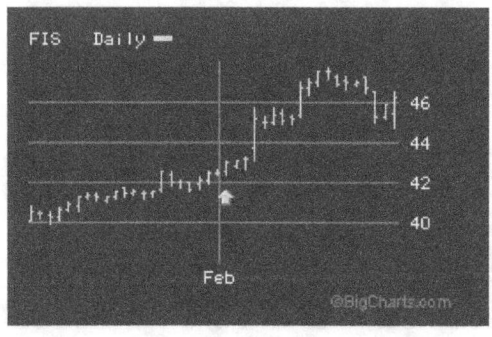

BXP   6/21/06

LUFK   3/7/06

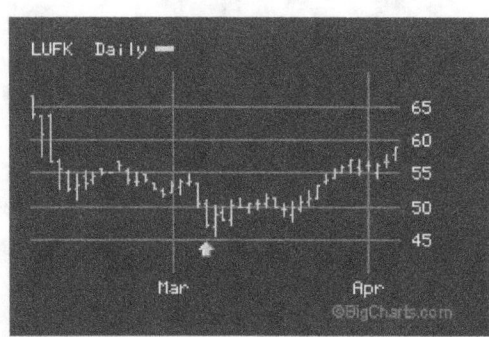

GVHR   1/18/06

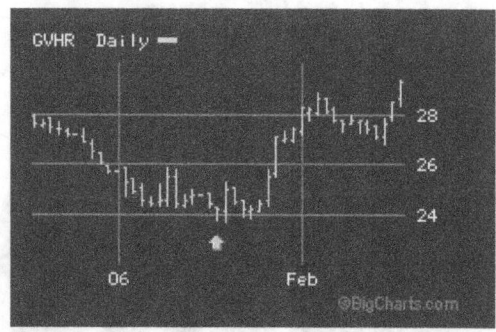

24

HUBG 1/5/06

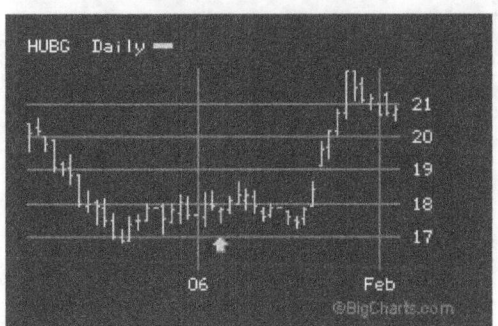

JOYG 11/18/05

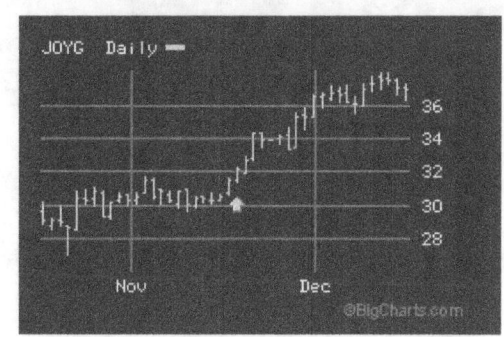

TKR 11/16/05

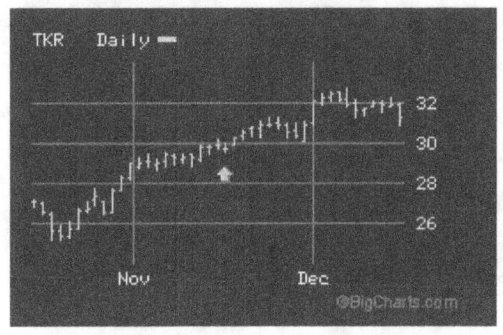

RRGB 10/27/05

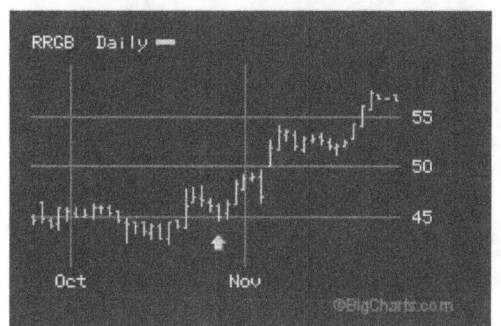

ACO 10/19/04

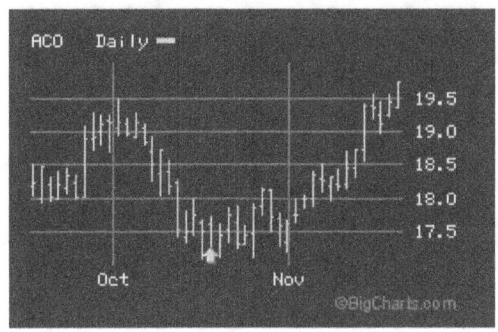

ADS 9/20/04

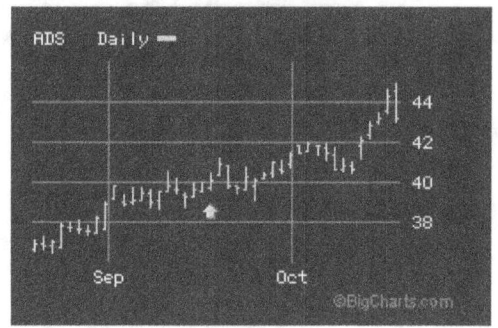

25

HAR   5/17/04

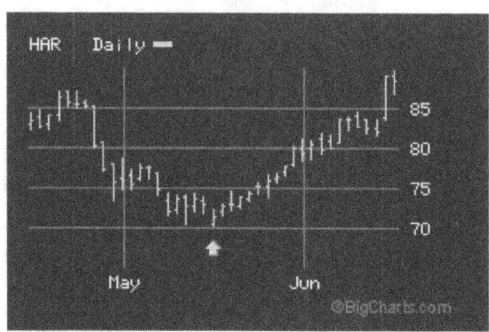

RGS   5/17/04

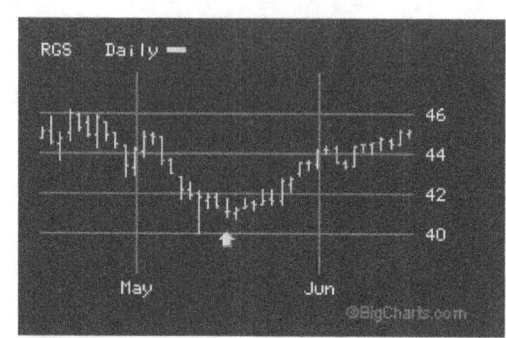

GB   11/21/03

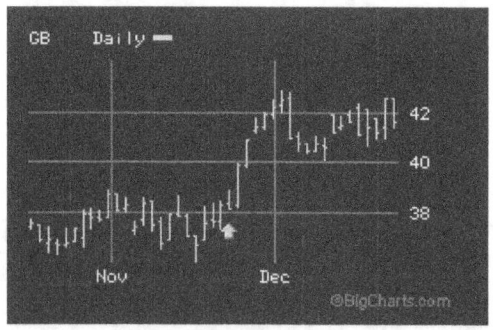

TOL   4/3/03

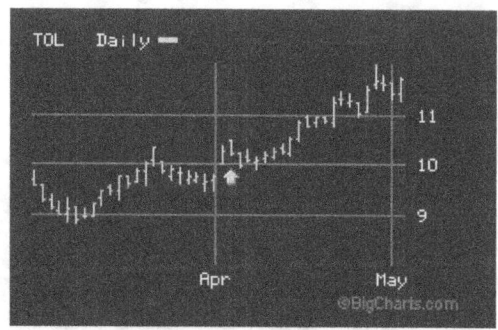

CUB   4/9/03

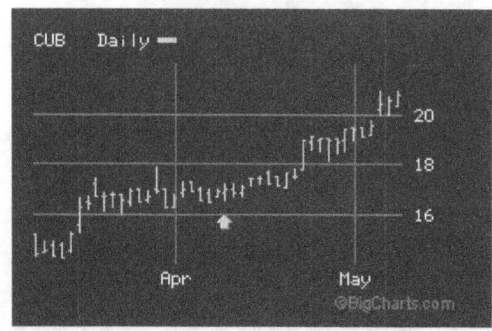

DGX   3/5/03

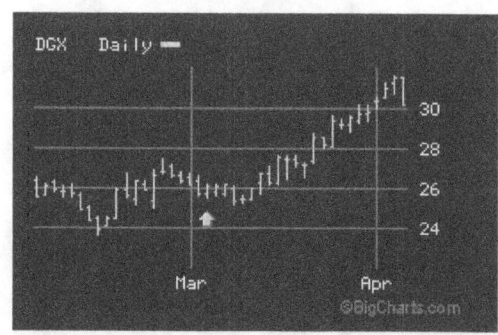

PLFE 2/12/02

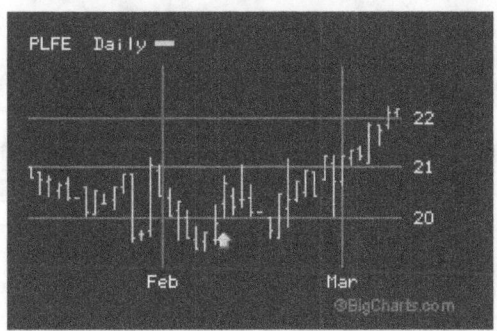

RTEC 2/20/02

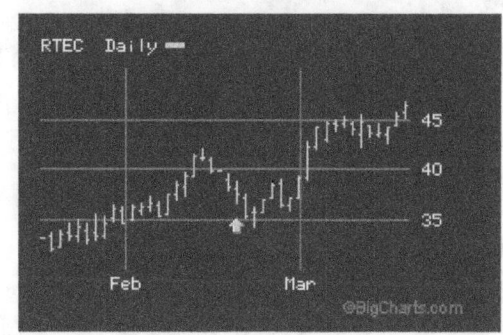

LAB 4/27/01

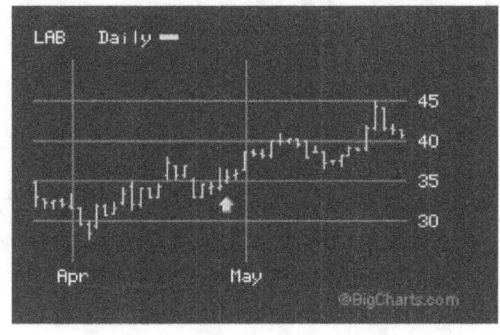

DCOM 11/21/01

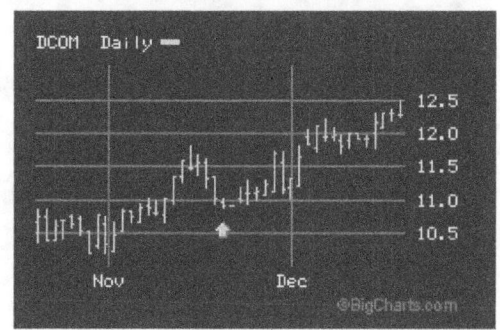

FED 4/2/01

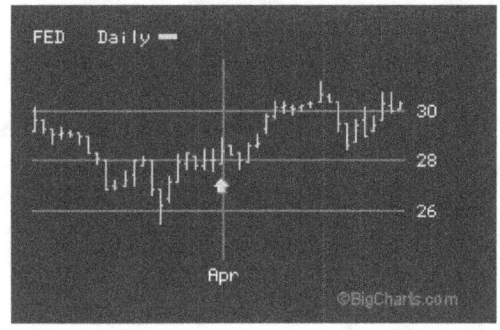

RLI 5/1/00

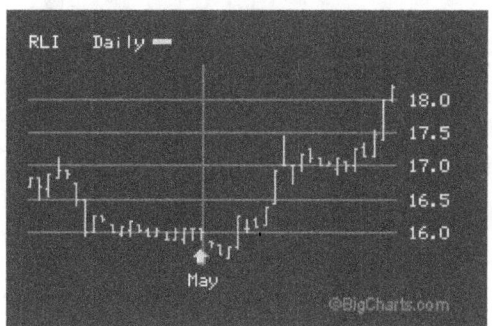

27

NVR 7/21/00

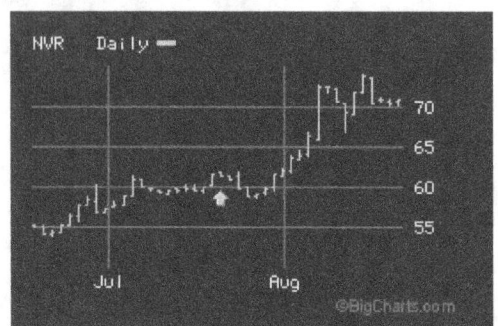

MXIM 7/28/00

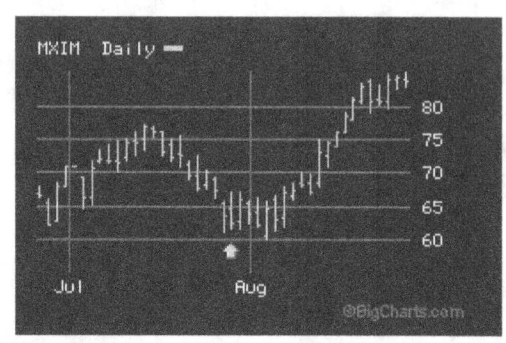

Chapter 5: Finding The Tailwind Stocks

Before you can trade the Tailwind stocks, you must first find them. The procedures in this chapter will take you step by step through the process of finding the Tailwind stocks.

When Standard & Poor's makes changes to their indexes, they issue a press release detailing the changes. They post the press release on their web site. According to Standard & Poor's, these announcements are made during the week after 5:15 PM Eastern Time[1]. The announcement will provide the details about which stocks will be added their index.

There are two steps to finding the Tailwind stocks. The first step is to find the announcements that detail the changes to the S&P indexes. The second step is to read the announcements and identify the Tailwind stocks. The procedures detailed in this chapter will take you through both of these steps so that you will be successful at uncovering the profits hiding in these Tailwind stocks.

Step 1 – Finding the Announcements

Go to Standard and Poor's website at www.standardandpoors.com. You will be taken to the homepage as shown in Example 1 below. Select your country and region as shown in the highlighted section on the screenshot. That will take you to the next page of the web site as shown in Example 2.

Example 1:

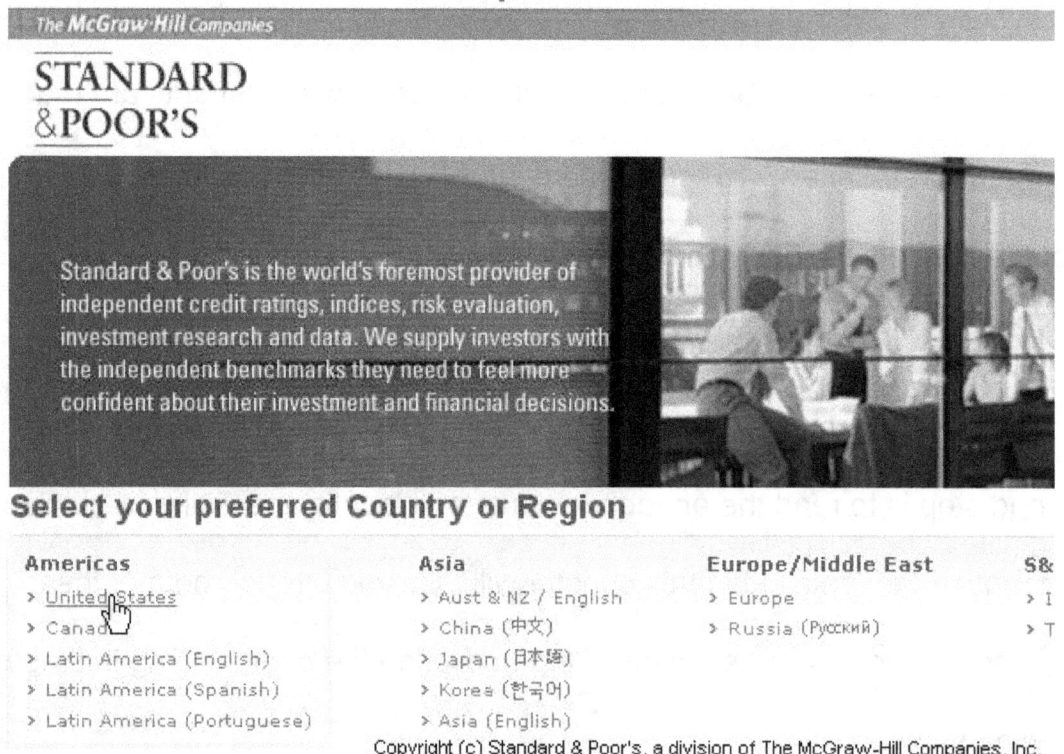

On the left side of this page you will see a heading that reads "Indices".

That section is highlighted in yellow on the screenshot. Click on that link.

That will take you to the next page of the web site as shown in Example 3.

Example 2:

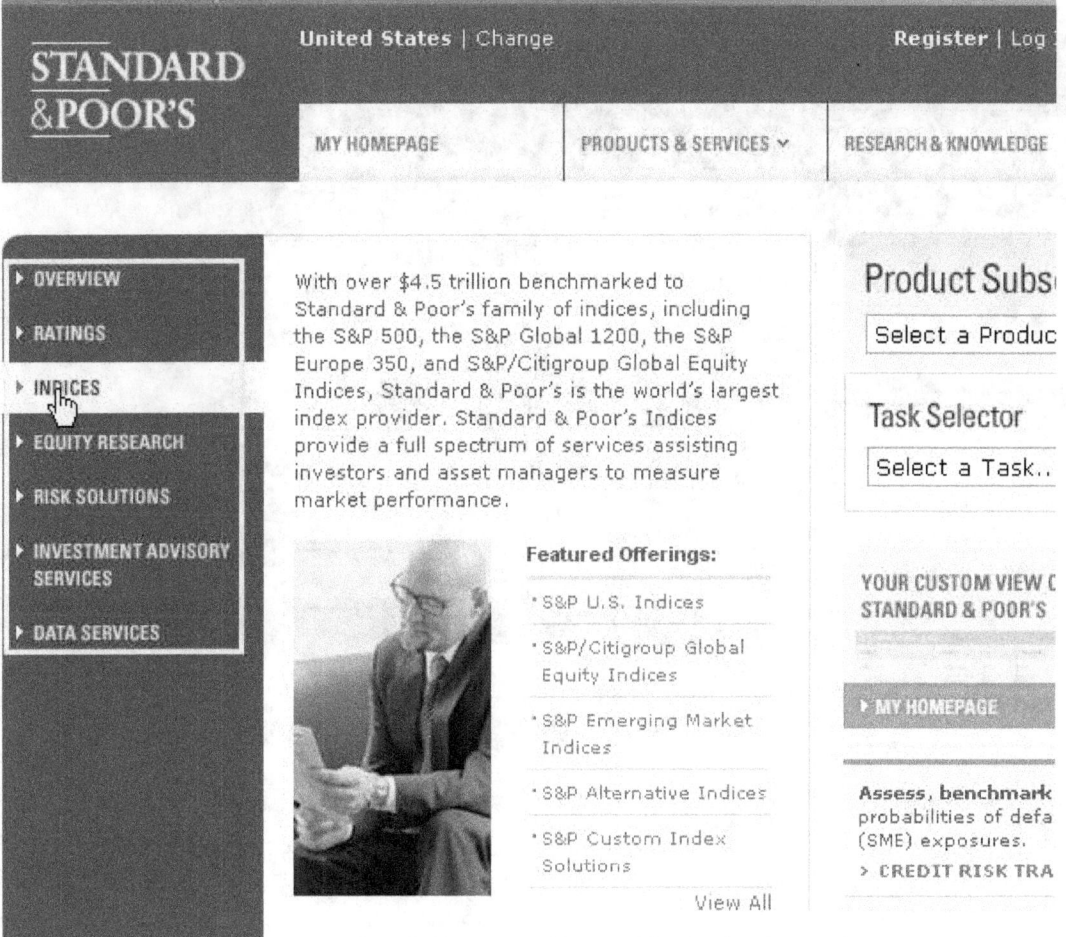

Copyright (c) Standard & Poor's, a division of The McGraw-Hill Companies, Inc.

On the left side of this page you will see a heading that reads "Indices Home". That section is highlighted in yellow on the screenshot. Under the "Indices Home" heading you will see a link that reads "Index News". Click on that link. That will take you to the next page of the web site as shown in Example 4.

Example 3:

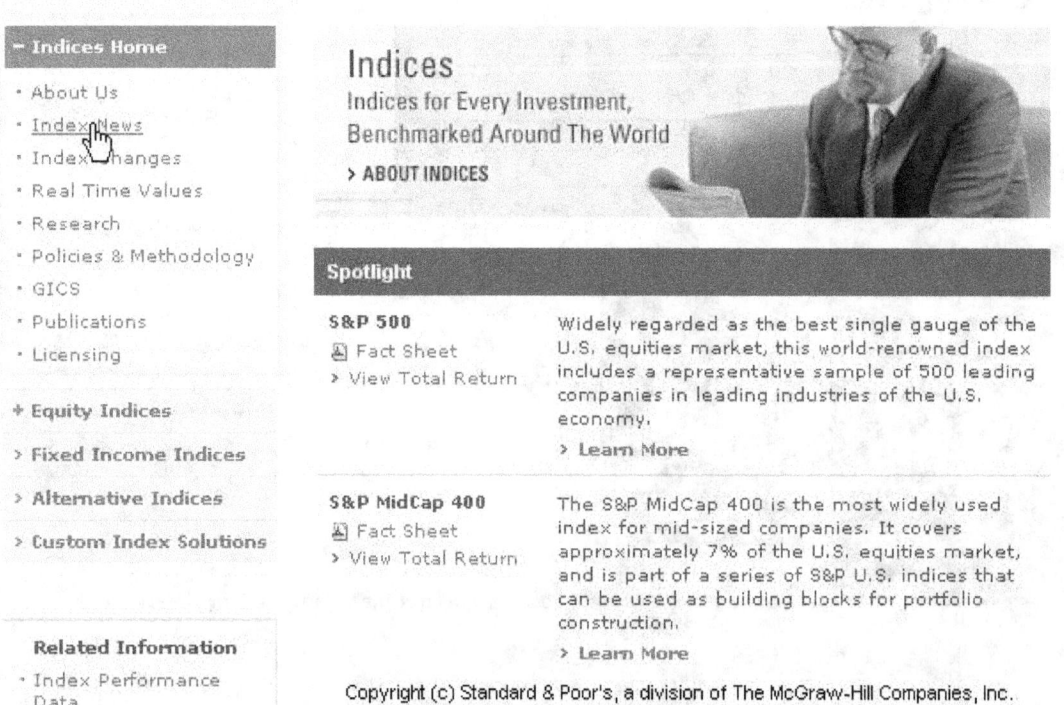

On this page, the announcements are posted in the center of the page under the "Indices News" heading. The section is highlighted on this screenshot. These are the S&P announcements that you are looking for. The announcement section shown here in Example 4 is shown in closer detail in Example 5.

Example 4:

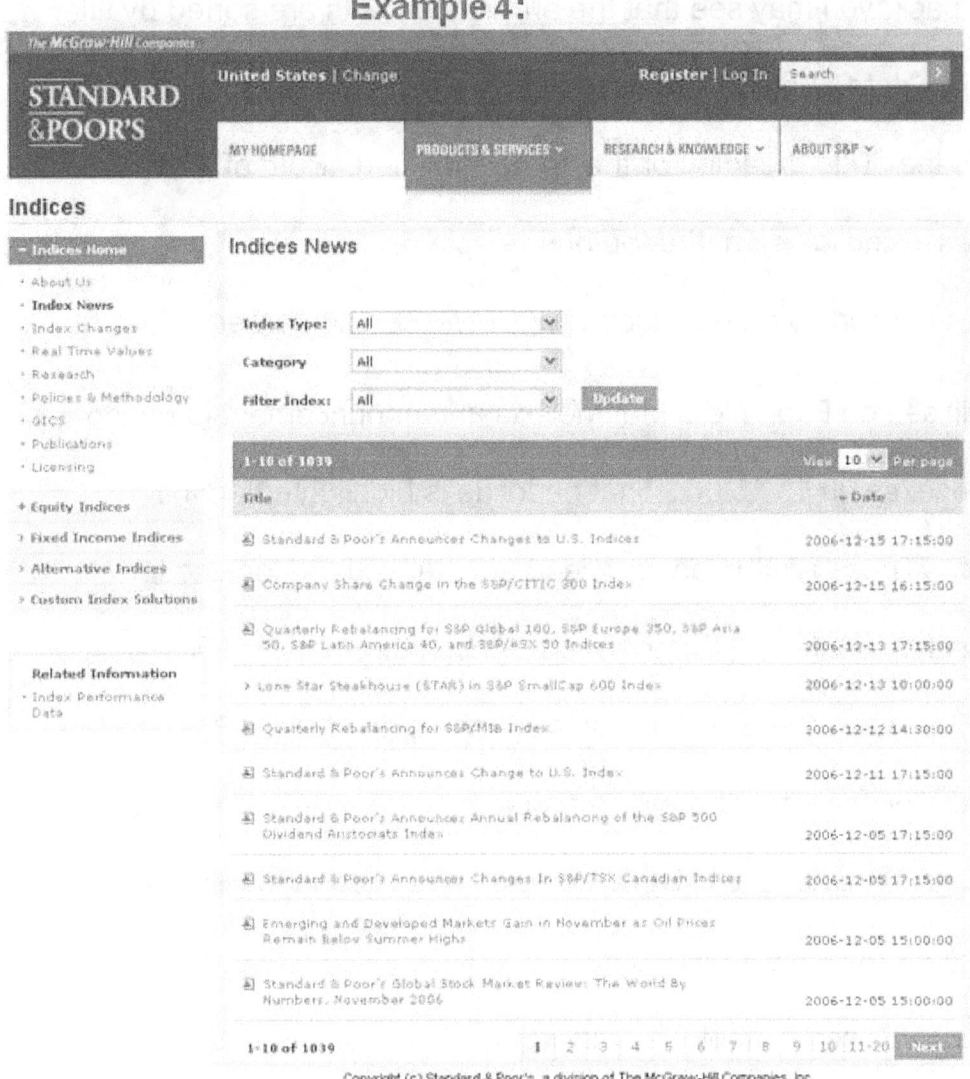

Example 5 is a larger view of the announcement section shown in Example 4. There are four parts highlighted on this screenshot.

When you view this page, you will see the most recent announcements first. You can page back through previous announcements by clicking on the page numbers that are highlighted at the bottom of Example 5. When you page back, you may see that the announcements are sorted by title instead of by date. You can adjust how the announcements are sorted by clicking on the "Title" heading or the "Date" heading. Both of these headings are highlighted at the top of Example 5. The "Date" heading enables you to sort by date in ascending or descending order.

You will see on Example 5 that there is an announcement of changes to the U.S. indexes on 12/15/06. That headline is highlighted on the screenshot. These are the announcements that you are looking for. You are looking for changes to Standard and Poor's three main U.S. indexes; the S&P 500 Index, the S&P MidCap 400 Index, and the S&P SmallCap 600 Index. You want to read any announcement that reads "Changes to U.S. Indices", "Changes to S&P 500 Index", and "Added to S&P MidCap 400 Index", or any variations or similar headings. You can see two more headings on this screenshot that you would also read. One is on 12/13/06,

"Lone Star Steakhouse in S&P SmallCap 600 Index", the other is on 12/11/06, "Standard & Poor's Announces Change To U.S. Index".

To read the announcement, you click on the headline. When you click on the headline that is highlighted in Example 5, you will see the announcement that is shown in Example 6.

Example 5:

1-10 of 1039	View 10 ∨ Per page
Title	▾ **Date**
Standard & Poor's Announces Changes to U.S. Indices	2006-12-15 17:15:00
Company Share Change in the S&P/CITIC 300 Index	2006-12-15 16:15:00
Quarterly Rebalancing for S&P Global 100, S&P Europe 350, S&P Asia 50, S&P Latin America 40, and S&P/ASX 50 Indices	2006-12-13 17:15:00
> Lone Star Steakhouse (STAR) in S&P SmallCap 600 Index	2006-12-13 10:00:00
Quarterly Rebalancing for S&P/MIB Index	2006-12-12 14:30:00
Standard & Poor's Announces Change to U.S. Index	2006-12-11 17:15:00
Standard & Poor's Announces Annual Rebalancing of the S&P 500 Dividend Aristocrats Index	2006-12-05 17:15:00
Standard & Poor's Announces Changes In S&P/TSX Canadian Indices	2006-12-05 17:15:00
Emerging and Developed Markets Gain in November as Oil Prices Remain Below Summer Highs	2006-12-05 15:00:00
Standard & Poor's Global Stock Market Review: The World By Numbers, November 2006	2006-12-05 15:00:00
1-10 of 1039	1 2 3 4 5 6 7 8 9 10 11-20 Next

When you click on a headline link as shown in Example 5, you will see

the S&P announcement as shown here in Example 6.

Example 6:

STANDARD
&POOR'S

Press Release

Standard & Poor's Announces Changes to U.S. Indices

New York, NY, December 15, 2006 – Standard & Poor's will make the following changes to the S&P 500 and S&P SmallCap 600 indices after the close of trading on Tuesday, December 19, 2006:

- Terex Corp. (NYSE:TEX) will replace Navistar International Corp. (NYSE:NAV) in the S&P 500. Navistar's common stock is scheduled to be delisted by the New York Stock Exchange prior to the open of trading on Wednesday, December 20.

- Mannatech Inc. (NASD:MTEX) will replace American Italian Pasta Co. (NYSE:PLB) in the S&P SmallCap 600. American Italian Pasta's common stock is scheduled to be delisted by the New York Stock Exchange prior to the open of trading on Wednesday, December 20.

Standard & Poor's will monitor these transactions, and post any relevant updates on its website: www.standardandpoors.com.

Terex manufactures a broad range of heavy-duty off-road trucks, mobile cranes and aerial work platforms. Headquartered in Westport, CT, the company will be added to the S&P 500 GICS (Global Industry Classification Standard) Construction & Farm Machinery & Heavy Trucks Sub-Industry index.

Mannatech develops proprietary nutritional supplements, topical products and weight-management products, primarily sold through a network-marketing system. Headquartered in Coppell, TX, the company will be added to the S&P 600 GICS Personal Products Sub-Industry index.

Copyright (c) Standard & Poor's, a division of The McGraw-Hill Companies, Inc.

You have now learned how to find the announcements. Follow these procedures in the evening to find the current announcements detailing changes to Standard and Poor's three main U.S. indexes; the S&P 500 Index, the S&P MidCap 400 Index, and the S&P SmallCap 600 Index. According to Standard & Poor's, the announcements are posted Monday night through Friday night at 5:15 PM Eastern Time. You can choose to check the Standard & Poor's web site each evening, or once a week, or once a month. After you have finished reading this entire book and have learned the Tailwind Trading System, you can decide how frequently you want to check the Standard & Poor's web site based on your schedule and trading habits.

Step 2 – Identifying the Tailwind Stocks

Once you have found an announcement detailing changes to the S&P 500 Index, the S&P MidCap 400 Index, or the S&P SmallCap 600 Index, the next step is to identify the Tailwind stocks. We will refer to the identification criteria detailed in this section as the Selection Criteria. Remember, the Tailwind stocks are those stocks that are <u>added</u> to the S&P 500 Index, the S&P MidCap 400 Index, and the S&P SmallCap 600 Index.

It is important to note that the announcements do not always use the words "add" or "added" when describing the action taken on a stock that is added to an index. The announcements will often use the word "replace". For the purposes of the Tailwind Trading System, "replace" means the same as "added" and these stocks are candidates for the Tailwind Trading System.

It is also important to note that some stocks are removed from one index, such as the S&P 500 Index, and transferred to a smaller index, like the S&P MidCap 400 Index. These stocks are not candidates for the Tailwind Trading System and should be avoided.

Also, some stocks are removed from a smaller index, like the SmallCap 600 Index, and transferred to a larger index, like the MidCap 400 Index. These stocks are candidates for the Tailwind Trading System.

When a stock is transferred from a larger index to a smaller index or from a smaller index to a larger index, the announcement will include the index that the stock is coming from and which index it is going to. For example, it may state that "S&P 500 component First Company will replace Second Company in the S&P MidCap 400 Index". This means that First Company will be removed from the S&P 500 Index and transferred to the

S&P MidCap 400 Index. You will be able to tell that this is a transfer

situation because the announcement will also state that a stock will be

added to the S&P 500 Index to take the place of First Company. In some

instances, the word "transfer" will be used in place of the word "replace".

The word "transfer" also means "added" for the Tailwind Trading System.

In order of size, the S&P 500 Index is the largest index, followed by the

S&P MidCap 400 Index, and then the S&P SmallCap 600 Index.

Further more, occasionally, a stock that is in the S&P REIT Composite

Index will be added to the S&P 500 Index, or the S&P MidCap 400 Index,

or the S&P SmallCap 600 Index. This is not the same situation as a stock

that is transferred from one index to another index as just described in the

previous paragraphs. A stock may be in both the S&P REIT Composite

Index and one of the three main U.S. S&P indexes; the S&P 500 Index, or

the S&P MidCap 400 Index, or the S&P SmallCap 600 Index. For example,

the announcement may state that "S&P REIT Composite constituent First

Company will replace Second Company in the S&P MidCap 400 Index".

This stock, First Company, is not removed from the S&P REIT Composite

Index and transferred to the S&P MidCap 400. First Company will remain

in the S&P REIT Composite Index and it will be added to the S&P MidCap

400 Index. These stocks <u>are</u> candidates for the Tailwind Trading System because they are added to either the S&P 500 Index, or the S&P MidCap 400 Index, or the S&P SmallCap 600 Index.

Also, sometimes the announcements will include changes specifically for the S&P REIT Composite Index. For example, the announcement may state that "Acme Hotels will replace Example Realty in the S&P REIT Composite Index". These stocks <u>are not</u> candidates for the Tailwind Trading System and should be avoided. You are only interested in stocks that are added to the S&P 500 Index, the S&P MidCap 400 Index, and the S&P SmallCap 600 Index.

There are several more situations that you should avoid. Stay away from mergers and acquisitions where the "new" company is replacing the "old" company in an index. For example, First Company is merging with Second Company to form FirstSecond Inc, and this new company is replacing First Company in an index. Essentially, the "new" company is replacing itself in the index. A similar situation occurs with some acquisitions. For example, Second Company may already be in an S&P index. First Company acquires Second Company, and First Company replaces Second Company in the S&P index. Again, essentially, the "new" company is replacing itself in the index. Avoid these types of mergers and

acquisitions; they <u>are not</u> candidates for the Tailwind Trading System.

There is one exception to this rule with mergers and acquisitions. If the

"new" company formed by the merger or acquisition is transferred to a

larger index, and not replacing itself in its current index, then it <u>is</u> a

candidate for the Tailwind Trading System.

Also, avoid spin-offs where the company being spun off will be added to

an index. These are companies with no track record and the stock usually

has not been issued yet when the S&P announcement is made.

Sometimes, you will see the ticker symbol in the S&P announcement with

the letters "wi" after it, meaning "when issued". For example, you may see

ticker symbol "XYZwi".

Included in the details about the index changes will be the date that the

changes are to take effect, commonly referred to as the effective date. The

effective date is an important part of the Tailwind Trading System, as you

will learn in **Chapter 7: Trading The Tailwind Stocks**. In some instances,

the announcement will not include an effective date. Instead, it will state

that the changes will take place on a date "To be announced". These

stocks may not be added to an index for a few weeks or even a month or more. These stocks <u>are not</u> candidates for the Tailwind Trading System and should be avoided.

Usually, a stock is added to an S&P index in one to seven business days from the day the announcement is released. Occasionally, the effective date may be more than seven business days from the day the announcement is released. These stocks <u>are not</u> candidates for the Tailwind Trading System and should be avoided. It is better to have a short time span from the announcement to the effective date so there is more of a buzz surrounding the stock. This will provide more opportunity for the stock price to rise and then drift lower by Day 56.

Occasionally, sometime after the initial announcement has been made, Standard & Poor's will change the effective date. They will post this notice in the same section where the announcements are posted. Watch for any date changes and keep track of the new effective date. If the new effective date is more than seven business days after the initial announcement or it has been changed to a date that is "To be announced", then it <u>is not</u> a candidate for the Tailwind Trading System and should be avoided.

The Selection Criteria can be summarized as follows:

1. Look for stocks that are <u>added</u> to the S&P 500 Index, MidCap 400 Index, and the SmallCap 600 Index, with these phrases or similar phrases:

- ❖ "add"
- ❖ "added"
- ❖ "replace"
- ❖ "transfer"

2. Look for stocks that are <u>added</u> to the S&P 500 Index, MidCap 400 Index, and the SmallCap 600 Index, including stocks that are:

- ❖ transferring from a smaller index to a larger index
- ❖ currently in the S&P REIT Composite Index

3. <u>Avoid</u> stocks that are added to an index when the stock to be added is:

- ❖ transferring from a larger index to a smaller index
- ❖ the result of a merger, when the "new" company replaces the "old" company in the same index
- ❖ the result of an acquisition, when the "new" company replaces the acquired company in the same index
- ❖ the result of a spin-off
- ❖ added on a date "to be announced"
- ❖ added on a date that is more than seven business days after the announcement is released

4. Watch for changes to the effective date.

Let's take a look at some examples of announcements and identify the Tailwind stocks. The text that identifies the stock as a Tailwind stock has been highlighted. Also, take note of the different headlines that have been used. These are the types of headlines you will look for when you follow the procedures outlined earlier in this chapter in **Step 1 – Finding the Announcements**.

Example 1 shows two stocks that were added to an S&P index. JAKK and BERW were added to the SmallCap 600 Index. JAKK and BERW are Tailwind stocks.

Example 1

JAKKS Pacific, Beringer Wine Estates Added to S&P SmallCap 600 Index

NEW YORK--(BUSINESS WIRE)--Jan. 5, 2000--Standard & Poor's will make the following changes in the S&P SmallCap 600 Index:

-    JAKKS Pacific (NASDAQ:JAKK) will replace Aquarion Co. (NYSE:WTR) in the S&P SmallCap 600 Index after the close of trading on Friday, January 7, 2000. Kelda Group PLC (not in an S&P Index) is acquiring Aquarion Co. in a transaction anticipated to become effective on that date.

-    Beringer Wine Estates (NASDAQ:BERW) will replace UST Corp. (NASDAQ:USTB) in the S&P SmallCap 600 Index after the close of trading on Tuesday, January 11, 2000. Citizens Financial Group, a subsidiary of Royal Bank of Scotland, is acquiring UST Corp. in a transaction anticipated to close on that date. The transaction is still subject to approval from the Massachusetts Board of Banking.
     Copyright © Business Wire

Example 2 shows a stock that was added to an S&P index. PVA was

added to the SmallCap 600 Index. PVA is a Tailwind stock.

Example 2

Standard & Poor's Announces Change to U.S. Index

New York, NY, February 15, 2005 – Penn Virginia Corp. (NYSE:PVA) will replace
Ionics Inc. (NYSE:ION) in the S&P SmallCap 600 after the close of trading on Tuesday,
February 22. Ionics is being acquired by a subsidiary of S&P 500 constituent General
Electric Co. (NYSE:GE) in a deal expected to close on or about that date, pending final
approval.
   Copyright © Standard & Poor's, a division of The McGraw-Hill Companies, Inc

Example 3 shows a stock that will be transferred from a <u>smaller</u> S&P index to a <u>larger</u> S&P index and a stock that will be added to an S&P index. BRL is transferring from the MidCap 400 Index to the S&P 500 Index to replace SFA. BRL is a Tailwind stock. Also, FNFG will be added to the MidCap 400 Index to replace BRL. FNFG is a Tailwind stock.

Example 3

Standard & Poor's Announces Changes to U.S. Indices

New York, NY, February 21, 2006 – S&P MidCap 400 constituent Barr Pharmaceuticals Inc. (NYSE:BRL) will replace Scientific-Atlanta Inc. (NYSE:SFA) in the S&P 500, and First Niagara Financial Group Inc. (NASD:FNFG) will replace Barr Pharmaceuticals in the S&P MidCap 400, after the close of trading on Friday, February 24. Scientific-Atlanta is being acquired by S&P 100 and S&P 500 constituent Cisco Systems Inc. (NASD:CSCO) in a deal expected to close on or about that date, pending final approval.
   Copyright © Standard & Poor's, a division of The McGraw-Hill Companies, Inc

Example 4 shows two stocks that will be transferred from <u>smaller</u> S&P indexes to <u>larger</u> S&P indexes and a stock that will be added to an S&P index. CVH is transferring from the MidCap 400 Index to the S&P 500 Index to replace MAY. CVH is a Tailwind stock. Also, TKR is transferring from the SmallCap 600 Index to the MidCap 400 Index to replace CVH. TKR is a Tailwind stock. ASVI will be added to the SmallCap 600 Index to replace TKR. ASVI is a Tailwind stock.

Example 4

Standard & Poor's Announces Changes to U.S. Indices

New York, NY, August 26, 2005 – Standard & Poor's will make the following changes to the S&P 500, S&P 100, S&P MidCap 400 and S&P SmallCap 600 indices after the close of trading on Monday, August 29:

S&P MidCap 400 constituent Coventry Health Care (NYSE:CVH) will replace May Department Stores Co. (NYSE:MAY) in the S&P 500. May is being acquired by S&P 500 constituent Federated Department Stores Inc. (NYSE:FD) in a deal expected to close on or about that date.

S&P SmallCap 600 constituent Timken Co. (NYSE:TKR) will replace Coventry Health in the S&P MidCap 400, and ASV Inc. (NASD:ASVI) will replace Timken in the S&P SmallCap 600.

Copyright © Standard & Poor's, a division of The McGraw-Hill Companies, Inc

Example 5 shows a spin-off stock that will be added to an S&P index and two stocks that will be transferred from <u>larger</u> S&P indexes to <u>smaller</u> S&P indexes. WUwi is a stock that is being spun off from FDC and will be added to the S&P 500 Index to replace ANDW. WUwi is <u>not</u> a Tailwind stock. ANDW is transferring from the S&P 500 Index to the MidCap 400 Index to replace CCMP. ANDW is <u>not</u> a Tailwind stock. Also, CCMP is transferring from the MidCap 400 Index to the SmallCap 600 Index to replace BFT. CCMP is <u>not</u> a Tailwind stock.

Example 5

Standard & Poor's Announces Changes to U.S. Indices

New York, NY, September 25, 2006 – Standard & Poor's will make the following changes to the S&P 500, MidCap 400 and SmallCap 600 indices:

The Western Union Company (NYSE:WUwi) will replace Andrew Corp. (NASD:ANDW) in the S&P 500, Andrew Corp. will replace Cabot Microelectronics Corp. (NASD:CCMP) in the S&P MidCap 400, and Cabot Microelectronics will replace Bally Total Fitness Holding Corp. (NYSE:BFT) in the S&P SmallCap 600 after the close of trading on Friday, September 29.

Western Union is being spun off by S&P 500 constituent First Data Corp. (NYSE:FDC) in a deal expected to close on or about that date. At today's close of trading Bally Total Fitness had a market capitalization of roughly $77 million, whereas the minimum market cap a company must maintain to be considered for addition to the S&P SmallCap 600 index is $300 million.

Copyright © Standard & Poor's, a division of The McGraw-Hill Companies, Inc

Example 6 shows a spin-off stock that will be added to an S&P index, a stock that will be transferred from a <u>smaller</u> S&P index to a <u>larger</u> S&P index, and a stock that will be transferred from a <u>larger</u> S&P index to a <u>smaller</u> S&P index. EW is a stock that is being spun off from BAX and will be added to the MidCap 400 Index to replace VRTS. EW is <u>not</u> a Tailwind stock. VRTS is transferring from the MidCap 400 Index to the S&P 500 Index to replace PBY. VRTS is a Tailwind stock. PBY is transferring from the S&P 500 Index to the SmallCap 600 Index to replace RURL. PBY is <u>not</u> a Tailwind stock.

Example 6

Standard & Poor's Announces Changes in S&P Indices

NEW YORK--(BUSINESS WIRE)--March 29, 2000--Standard & Poor's will make the following changes in the S&P 500, S&P MidCap 400 and S&P SmallCap 600 Indices:

-- Edwards Lifesciences Corp. (NYSE:EW) will replace Veritas Software (NASDAQ:VRTS) in the S&P MidCap 400 Index after the close of trading on Friday, March 31, 2000.. S&P 500 component Baxter International (NYSE:BAX) is spinning off Edwards Lifesciences Corp. to BAX shareholders.

-- Veritas Software (NASDAQ:VRTS) will replace Pep Boys (NYSE:PBY) in the S&P 500 Index after the close of trading on Friday, March 31, 2000. Pep Boys (NYSE:PBY) will replace Rural/Metro Corp. (RURL) in the S&P SmallCap 600 Index. Rural/Metro Corp. is being removed for lack of representation.
Copyright © Business Wire

Example 7 shows two companies that are merging and the new

company is replacing the old company in an S&P index. DYN is merging

with ILN, and the new company, DYN, will replace the old company, ILN, in

the MidCap 400 Index. DYN is <u>not</u> a Tailwind stock.

Example 7

Standard & Poor's Announces Changes in S&P Indices

NEW YORK--(BUSINESS WIRE)--January 31, 2000--Standard & Poor's will make the following changes in the S&P MidCap 400, S&P SmallCap 600 and S&P REIT Composite Indices:

-- Dynegy Inc. (New) (NYSE:DYN) will replace Illinova Corp. (NYSE:ILN) in the S&P MidCap 400 Index after the close of trading on Tuesday, February 1, 2000. Illinova Corp. and Dynegy Inc. (Old) are merging into one company. The transaction is anticipated to close on that date.
   Copyright © Business Wire

Example 8 shows a company acquiring a company that is in an S&P

index and it will replace the acquired company in the S&P index. PSTI is

acquiring NDC, a stock that is already in the SmallCap 600 Index, and

PSTI will replace NDC in the SmallCap 600. PSTI is <u>not</u> a Tailwind stock.

Example 8

Standard & Poor's Announces Changes to U.S. Indices

New York, NY, January 3, 2006 – Standard & Poor's will make the following change to the S&P SmallCap 600 indices:

- Per-Se Technologies Inc. (NASD:PSTI) will replace NDCHealth Corp. (NYSE:NDC) in the S&P SmallCap 600 after the close of trading on Friday, January 6. Per-Se is acquiring NDCHealth in a deal expected to close on or about that date, pending final approvals.
　　Copyright © Standard & Poor's, a division of The McGraw-Hill Companies, Inc

Example 9 shows a stock that was added to an S&P index on a date to be announced. HAIN will be added to the SmallCap 600 Index; however, the change will take place on a date to be announced. HAIN is <u>not</u> a Tailwind stock.

Example 9

Hain Food Group Added to S&P SmallCap 600 Index

NEW YORK, N.Y.--(BUSINESS WIRE)--Feb. 1, 2000--Standard & Poor's will replace RailTex Inc. (NASDAQ:RTEX) in the S&P SmallCap 600 Index with Hain Food Group (NASDAQ:HAIN) after the close of trading on a date to be announced. RailAmerica Inc. (NASDAQ:RAIL) is acquiring RailTex Inc. RailAmerica Inc. will not be added to an S&P Index at this time.
  Copyright © Business Wire

Example 10 shows several stocks that were added to an S&P index on a date to be announced. MTB, CEPH, and SCSS will be added to the S&P 500 Index, MidCap 400 Index, and the SmallCap 600 Index respectively. However, the change will take place on a date to be announced. MTB, CEPH, and SCSS are <u>not</u> Tailwind stocks.

Example 10

Standard & Poor's Announces Changes To S&P U.S. Indices

New York, NY, February 23, 2004 – Standard & Poor's will make the following changes to the S&P 500, S&P MidCap 400 and S&P SmallCap 600 Indices after the close of trading on a date to be announced:

• S&P MidCap 400 constituent M&T Bank Corp. (NYSE:MTB) will replace Concord EFS Inc. (NYSE:CE) in the S&P 500. Concord EFS is being acquired by fellow S&P 500 constituent First Data Corp. (NYSE:FDC), in a transaction that is still pending shareholder approval. S&P SmallCap 600 constituent Cephalon Inc. (NASD:CEPH) will replace M&T Bank in the S&P MidCap 400, while Select Comfort Corp. (NASD:SCSS) will replace Cephalon in the S&P SmallCap 600.
    Copyright © Standard & Poor's, a division of The McGraw-Hill Companies, Inc

Chapter 6:   Test Your Skills; Identify The Tailwind Stocks

This chapter will help you identify the Tailwind stocks in the Standard & Poor's announcements. Each Standard & Poor's announcement in this chapter is a test. Read the Standard & Poor's announcement and write down the ticker symbol of each stock that you think is a Tailwind stock. Also, write down the effective date. The answer for each test is shown just below the test. When you are looking at each page, just look at the upper part of the page where the test is, so you will not see the correct answer until you have written down your answer.

Reminder, the Selection Criteria is as follows:

Look for stocks that are <u>added</u> to the S&P 500 Index, MidCap 400 Index, and the SmallCap 600 Index, with these phrases or similar phrases:

- ❖ "add"
- ❖ "added"
- ❖ "replace"
- ❖ "transfer"

Look for stocks that are <u>added</u> to the S&P 500 Index, MidCap 400 Index, and the SmallCap 600 Index, including stocks that are:

- ❖ transferring from a smaller index to a larger index
- ❖ currently in the S&P REIT Composite Index

<u>Avoid</u> stocks that are added to an index when the stock to be added is:

- ❖ transferring from a larger index to a smaller index
- ❖ the result of a merger, when the "new" company replaces the "old" company in the same index
- ❖ the result of an acquisition, when the "new" company replaces the acquired company in the same index
- ❖ the result of a spin-off
- ❖ added on a date "to be announced"
- ❖ added on a date that is more than seven business days after the announcement is released

Test 1

Standard & Poor's Announces Changes to S&P U.S. Indices

New York, NY, March 25, 2004 –

- S&P MidCap 400 constituent E*TRADE Financial Corp. (NYSE:ET) will replace FleetBoston Financial Corp. (NYSE:FBF) in the S&P 500 after the close of trading on Wednesday, March 31, 2004. FleetBoston Financial is being acquired by fellow S&P 500 constituent Banc of America Corp. (NYSE:BAC) in a transaction anticipated to close on or about that date.

- S&P SmallCap 600 constituent Ryland Group Inc. (NYSE:RYL) will replace E*TRADE Financial in the S&P MidCap 400, while Sterling Financial Corp. (NASD:STSA) will replace Ryland Group in the S&P SmallCap 600.

    Copyright © Standard & Poor's, a division of The McGraw-Hill Companies, Inc

Answer 1

Standard & Poor's Announces Changes to S&P U.S. Indices

New York, NY, March 25, 2004 –

- S&P MidCap 400 constituent E*TRADE Financial Corp. (NYSE:ET) will replace FleetBoston Financial Corp. (NYSE:FBF) in the S&P 500 after the close of trading on Wednesday, March 31, 2004. FleetBoston Financial is being acquired by fellow S&P 500 constituent Banc of America Corp. (NYSE:BAC) in a transaction anticipated to close on or about that date.

- S&P SmallCap 600 constituent Ryland Group Inc. (NYSE:RYL) will replace E*TRADE Financial in the S&P MidCap 400, while Sterling Financial Corp. (NASD:STSA) will replace Ryland Group in the S&P SmallCap 600.

    Copyright © Standard & Poor's, a division of The McGraw-Hill Companies, Inc

Answer – ET, RYL, and STSA are Tailwind stocks. ET and RYL are transferring from smaller indexes to larger indexes. ET is transferring from the MidCap 400 Index to the S&P 500 Index, replacing FBF. RYL is transferring from the SmallCap 600 Index to the MidCap400 Index, replacing ET. STSA will be added to the SmallCap 600 Index, replacing RYL. The date they will be added to their respective indexes is 3/31/04.

Test 2

Standard & Poor's Announces Changes to S&P Indices

New York, NY, October 25, 2004 – Standard & Poor's will make the following changes to the S&P 500 and S&P SmallCap 600 Indices:

• Laboratory Corporation of America Holdings (NYSE:LH) will replace SouthTrust Corp. (NASD:SOTR) in the S&P 500 after the close of trading on a date to be announced. SouthTrust is being acquired by fellow S&P 500 constituent Wachovia Corp. (NYSE:WB) in a deal is still subject to shareholder approval.

• CIT Group Inc. (NYSE:CIT) will replace AT&T Wireless Services Inc. (NYSE:AWE) in the S&P 500 after the close of trading on a date to be announced. AT&T Wireless is being acquired by Cingular Wireless in a transaction still subject to final approvals.

• Parkway Properties Inc. (NYSE:PKY) will replace Community First Bankshares Inc. (NASD:CFBX) in the S&P SmallCap 600 after the close of trading on Friday, October 29. Community First is being acquired by BancWest Corp. in a deal expected to close on or about that date.
    Copyright © Standard & Poor's, a division of The McGraw-Hill Companies, Inc

Answer 2

Standard & Poor's Announces Changes to S&P Indices

New York, NY, October 25, 2004 – Standard & Poor's will make the following changes to the S&P 500 and S&P SmallCap 600 Indices:

• Laboratory Corporation of America Holdings (NYSE:LH) will replace SouthTrust Corp. (NASD:SOTR) in the S&P 500 after the close of trading on a date to be announced. SouthTrust is being acquired by fellow S&P 500 constituent Wachovia Corp. (NYSE:WB) in a deal is still subject to shareholder approval.

• CIT Group Inc. (NYSE:CIT) will replace AT&T Wireless Services Inc. (NYSE:AWE) in the S&P 500 after the close of trading on a date to be announced. AT&T Wireless is being acquired by Cingular Wireless in a transaction still subject to final approvals.

• Parkway Properties Inc. (NYSE:PKY) will replace Community First Bankshares Inc. (NASD:CFBX) in the S&P SmallCap 600 after the close of trading on Friday, October 29. Community First is being acquired by BancWest Corp. in a deal expected to close on or about that date.
    Copyright © Standard & Poor's, a division of The McGraw-Hill Companies, Inc

Answer – LH and CIT are not Tailwind stocks. They will be added to the S&P 500 Index on dates to be announced. PKY is a Tailwind stock. It will be added to the SmallCap 600 Index, replacing CFBX. The date PKY will be added is 10/29/04

Test 3

eLoyalty Corporation, Cohu Inc. Added to S&P Smallcap 600 Index

NEW YORK--(BUSINESS WIRE)--Feb. 14, 2000--Standard & Poor's will make the following changes in the S&P Smallcap 600 Index after the close of trading on Tuesday, February 15, 2000:

-   eLoyalty Corporation (NASDAQ:ELOY) will replace Technology Solutions (NASDAQ:TSCC) in the S&P SmallCap 600 Index. Technology Solutions is spinning off eLoyalty Corp., its e-solution and enterprise customer management division, to its shareholders.

- Cohu Inc. (NASDAQ:COHU) will replace Southern Energy Homes (NASDAQ:SEHI) in the S&P SmallCap 600 Index. Southern Energy Homes is being removed for lack of representation.
   Copyright © Business Wire

Answer 3

eLoyalty Corporation, Cohu Inc. Added to S&P Smallcap 600 Index

NEW YORK--(BUSINESS WIRE)--Feb. 14, 2000--Standard & Poor's will make the following changes in the S&P Smallcap 600 Index after the close of trading on Tuesday, February 15, 2000:

-   eLoyalty Corporation (NASDAQ:ELOY) will replace Technology Solutions (NASDAQ:TSCC) in the S&P SmallCap 600 Index. Technology Solutions is spinning off eLoyalty Corp., its e-solution and enterprise customer management division, to its shareholders.

- Cohu Inc. (NASDAQ:COHU) will replace Southern Energy Homes (NASDAQ:SEHI) in the S&P SmallCap 600 Index. Southern Energy Homes is being removed for lack of representation.
   Copyright © Business Wire

Answer – ELOY is not a Tailwind stock. It is a spin-off stock. COHU is a Tailwind stock. It will be added to the SmallCap 600 Index. The date COHU will be added is 2/15/00.

Test 4

Standard & Poor's Announces Changes to U.S. Indices

New York, NY, March 21, 2005 – Standard & Poor's will make the following change to the S&P 500 after the close of trading on Thursday, March 24:

• S&P 500 constituent Sears, Roebuck & Co. (NYSE:S) is merging with Kmart Holding Corp. (NASD:KMRT) in a deal subject to shareholder approval. The surviving company, Sears Holdings Corp. (NASD:SHLD), will replace Sears Roebuck in the S&P 500.
   Copyright © Standard & Poor's, a division of The McGraw-Hill Companies, Inc

Answer 4

Standard & Poor's Announces Changes to U.S. Indices

New York, NY, March 21, 2005 – Standard & Poor's will make the following change to the S&P 500 after the close of trading on Thursday, March 24:

• S&P 500 constituent Sears, Roebuck & Co. (NYSE:S) is merging with Kmart Holding Corp. (NASD:KMRT) in a deal subject to shareholder approval. The surviving company, Sears Holdings Corp. (NASD:SHLD), will replace Sears Roebuck in the S&P 500.
   Copyright © Standard & Poor's, a division of The McGraw-Hill Companies, Inc

Answer – There are no Tailwind stocks here. S and KMRT are merging to form SHLD. SHLD will replace S in the S&P 500 Index, essentially replacing itself.

Test 5

Standard & Poor's Announces Changes to U.S. Indices

New York, NY, December 15, 2006 – Standard & Poor's will make the following changes to the S&P 500 and S&P SmallCap 600 indices after the close of trading on Tuesday, December 19,2006:

• Terex Corp. (NYSE:TEX) will replace Navistar International Corp. (NYSE:NAV) in the S&P 500. Navistar's common stock is scheduled to be delisted by the New York Stock Exchange prior to the open of trading on Wednesday, December 20.

• Mannatech Inc. (NASD:MTEX) will replace American Italian Pasta Co. (NYSE:PLB) in the S&P SmallCap 600. American Italian Pasta's common stock is scheduled to be delisted by the New York Stock Exchange prior to the open of trading on Wednesday, December 20.
   Copyright © Standard & Poor's, a division of The McGraw-Hill Companies, Inc

Answer 5

Standard & Poor's Announces Changes to U.S. Indices

New York, NY, December 15, 2006 – Standard & Poor's will make the following changes to the S&P 500 and S&P SmallCap 600 indices after the close of trading on Tuesday, December 19,2006:

• Terex Corp. (NYSE:TEX) will replace Navistar International Corp. (NYSE:NAV) in the S&P 500. Navistar's common stock is scheduled to be delisted by the New York Stock Exchange prior to the open of trading on Wednesday, December 20.

• Mannatech Inc. (NASD:MTEX) will replace American Italian Pasta Co. (NYSE:PLB) in the S&P SmallCap 600. American Italian Pasta's common stock is scheduled to be delisted by the New York Stock Exchange prior to the open of trading on Wednesday, December 20.
   Copyright © Standard & Poor's, a division of The McGraw-Hill Companies, Inc

Answer – TEX and MTEX are Tailwind stocks. TEX will be added the S&P 500 Index, replacing NAV. MTEX will be added to the SmallCap 600 Index, replacing PLB. The date that TEX and MTEX will be added to their respective indexes is 12/19/06.

Test 6

Standard & Poor's Announces Changes to U.S. Indices

New York, NY, November 2, 2006 – Standard & Poor's will make the following changes to the S&P 500, S&P MidCap 400 and S&P SmallCap 600 indices:

• S&P 500 constituent Louisiana-Pacific Corp. (NYSE:LPX) will replace Fidelity National Information Services Inc. (NYSE:FIS) in the S&P MidCap 400, Fidelity National Information Services Inc. will replace Louisiana-Pacific Corp. in the S&P 500, and Nuveen Investments Inc. (NYSE:JNC) will replace Fidelity National Financial Inc. (NYSE:FNF) in the S&P MidCap 400 after the close of trading on Thursday, November 9. Fidelity National Financial is being acquired by Fidelity National Information Services in a deal expected to close on or about that date, pending final approvals.
   Copyright © Standard & Poor's, a division of The McGraw-Hill Companies, Inc

Answer 6

Standard & Poor's Announces Changes to U.S. Indices

New York, NY, November 2, 2006 – Standard & Poor's will make the following changes to the S&P 500, S&P MidCap 400 and S&P SmallCap 600 indices:

• <u>S&P 500 constituent Louisiana-Pacific Corp. (NYSE:LPX) will replace Fidelity National Information Services Inc. (NYSE:FIS) in the S&P MidCap 400</u>, Fidelity National Information Services Inc. (NYSE:FIS) will replace Louisiana-Pacific Corp. in the S&P 500, and Nuveen Investments Inc. (NYSE:JNC) will replace Fidelity National Financial Inc. (NYSE:FNF) in the S&P MidCap 400 after the close of trading on Thursday, November 9. Fidelity National Financial (NYSE:FNF) is being acquired by Fidelity National Information Services (NYSE:FIS) in a deal expected to close on or about that date, pending final approvals.
   Copyright © Standard & Poor's, a division of The McGraw-Hill Companies, Inc

Answer – LPX is not a Tailwind stock. LPX is being transferred from a larger index to a smaller index, from the S&P 500 Index to the MidCap 400 Index. FIS is a Tailwind stock. FIS is acquiring FNF; however, it is not replacing itself in an index. FIS is being transferred from a smaller index to a larger index, from the MidCap 400 Index to the S&P 500 Index. JNC is a Tailwind stock. JNC will be added to the MidCap 400 Index, replacing FNF. The date FIS and JNC will be added to their respective indexes is 11/9/06.

Test 7

Staten Island Bancorp Added To S&P SmallCap 600 Index

NEW YORK--(BUSINESS WIRE)--Jan. 12, 2000--Standard & Poor's will replace Premier Bancshares (NYSE:PMB) in the S&P SmallCap 600 Index with Staten Island Bancorp (NYSE:SIB) after the close of trading on Wednesday, January 13, 2000. S&P 500 component BB&T Corp. is acquiring Premier Bancshares in a transaction anticipated to close on that date.

     Copyright © Business Wire

Answer 7

Staten Island Bancorp Added To S&P SmallCap 600 Index

NEW YORK--(BUSINESS WIRE)--Jan. 12, 2000--Standard & Poor's will replace Premier Bancshares (NYSE:PMB) in the S&P SmallCap 600 Index with Staten Island Bancorp (NYSE:SIB) after the close of trading on Wednesday, January 13, 2000. S&P 500 component BB&T Corp. is acquiring Premier Bancshares in a transaction anticipated to close on that date.

     Copyright © Business Wire

     Answer – SIB is a Tailwind stock. SIB will be added to the SmallCap 600 Index, replacing PMB. The date SIB will be added to the index is 1/13/00.

Test 8

Standard & Poor's Announces Changes to U.S. Indices

New York, NY, March 7, 2006 – S&P SmallCap 600 constituent Florida Rock Industries Inc. (NYSE:FRK) will replace Inamed Corp. (NASD:IMDC) in the S&P MidCap 400, and Genesis HealthCare Corp. (NASD:GHCI) will replace Florida Rock in the S&P SmallCap 600, after the close of trading on a date to be announced. Inamed is being acquired by S&P 500 constituent Allergan Inc. (NYSE:AGN) in a deal that could be completed as soon as after this Friday's close of trading, pending the approval of the Federal Trade Commission and shareholders.
   Copyright © Standard & Poor's, a division of The McGraw-Hill Companies, Inc

Answer 8

Standard & Poor's Announces Changes to U.S. Indices

New York, NY, March 7, 2006 – S&P SmallCap 600 constituent Florida Rock Industries Inc. (NYSE:FRK) will replace Inamed Corp. (NASD:IMDC) in the S&P MidCap 400, and Genesis HealthCare Corp. (NASD:GHCI) will replace Florida Rock in the S&P SmallCap 600, after the close of trading on a date to be announced. Inamed is being acquired by S&P 500 constituent Allergan Inc. (NYSE:AGN) in a deal that could be completed as soon as after this Friday's close of trading, pending the approval of the Federal Trade Commission and shareholders.
   Copyright © Standard & Poor's, a division of The McGraw-Hill Companies, Inc

Answer – There are no Tailwind stocks here. FRK and GHCI will be added to indexes; however, they will be added on a date to be announced.

Test 9

Standard & Poor's Announces Changes to U.S. Indices

New York, NY, December 20, 2006 – Standard & Poor's will make the following changes to the S&P 500, S&P MidCap 400, and S&P SmallCap 600 indices:

• Spectra Energy Corp. (NYSE:SEwi) will replace Parametric Technology Corp. (NASD:PMTC) in the S&P 500, and Parametric Technology will replace Pier 1 Imports Inc. (NYSE:PIR) in the S&P MidCap 400 after the close of trading on Friday, December 29. Spectra Energy is being spun off by S&P 500 constituent Duke Energy Corp. (NYSE:DUK) in a transaction expected to close on or about that date. At today's close of trading Pier 1 had a market capitalization of approximately $556 million, ranking 400th in the index.

• Movado Group Inc. (NYSE:MOV) will replace Connetics Corporation (NASD:CNCT) in the S&P SmallCap 600 index after the close of trading on a date to be announced. Connetics is being acquired by Stiefel Laboratories Inc. in a deal that is still pending final approvals.
  Copyright © Standard & Poor's, a division of The McGraw-Hill Companies, Inc

Answer 9

Standard & Poor's Announces Changes to U.S. Indices

New York, NY, December 20, 2006 – Standard & Poor's will make the following changes to the S&P 500, S&P MidCap 400, and S&P SmallCap 600 indices:

• <u>Spectra Energy Corp. (NYSE:SEwi) will replace Parametric Technology Corp. (NASD:PMTC) in the S&P 500, and Parametric Technology will replace Pier 1 Imports Inc. (NYSE:PIR) in the S&P MidCap 400</u> after the close of trading on Friday, December 29. <u>Spectra Energy is being spun off</u> by S&P 500 constituent Duke Energy Corp. (NYSE:DUK) in a transaction expected to close on or about that date. At today's close of trading Pier 1 had a market capitalization of approximately $556 million, ranking 400th in the index.

• <u>Movado Group Inc. (NYSE:MOV) will replace</u> Connetics Corporation (NASD:CNCT) in the S&P SmallCap 600 index after the close of trading <u>on a date to be announced</u>. Connetics is being acquired by Stiefel Laboratories Inc. in a deal that is still pending final approvals.
  Copyright © Standard & Poor's, a division of The McGraw-Hill Companies, Inc

Answer – There are no Tailwind stocks here. SEwi is a spin-off stock. PMTC is being transferred from a larger index to a smaller index, from the S&P 500 Index to the MidCap 400 Index. PIR is being removed from the MidCap 400 Index and will not be added to another S&P index. MOV will be added to the SmallCap 600 Index on a date to be announced.

Test 10

Standard & Poor's Announces Changes in S&P U.S. Indices

NEW YORK, March 24 /PRNewswire/ -- Standard & Poor's will make the following changes in the S&P 500, S&P MidCap 400 and S&P SmallCap 600 Indices:

* S&P MidCap 400 component Symantec Corp. (Nasdaq: SYMC) will replace Household International Inc. (NYSE: HI) in the S&P 500 Index after the close of trading on Friday, March 28, 2003. S&P Global 1200 constituent HSBC Holdings Plc (NYSE: HBC) is acquiring Household International in a transaction scheduled to close on or about that date. The deal still needs regulatory and shareholder approval. S&P SmallCap 600 constituent Fair Isaac & Co. (NYSE: FIC) will replace Symantec Corp. in the S&P MidCap 400 Index, while Flowers Foods Inc. (NYSE: FLO) will replace Fair Isaac & Co. in the S&P SmallCap 600 Index.

Copyright © PRNewswire

Answer 10

Standard & Poor's Announces Changes in S&P U.S. Indices

NEW YORK, March 24 /PRNewswire/ -- Standard & Poor's will make the following changes in the S&P 500, S&P MidCap 400 and S&P SmallCap 600 Indices:

* S&P MidCap 400 component Symantec Corp. (Nasdaq: SYMC) will replace Household International Inc. (NYSE: HI) in the S&P 500 Index after the close of trading on Friday, March 28, 2003. S&P Global 1200 constituent HSBC Holdings Plc (NYSE: HBC) is acquiring Household International in a transaction scheduled to close on or about that date. The deal still needs regulatory and shareholder approval. S&P SmallCap 600 constituent Fair Isaac & Co. (NYSE: FIC) will replace Symantec Corp. in the S&P MidCap 400 Index, while Flowers Foods Inc. (NYSE: FLO) will replace Fair Isaac & Co. in the S&P SmallCap 600 Index.

Copyright © PRNewswire

Answer – SYMC, FIC, and FLO are Tailwind stocks. SYMC and FIC are transferring from smaller indexes to larger indexes. SYMC is transferring from the MidCap 400 Index to the S&P 500 Index, replacing HI. FIC is transferring from the SmallCap 600 Index to the MidCap400 Index, replacing SYMC. FLO will be added to the SmallCap 600 Index, replacing FIC. The date they will be added to their respective indexes is 3/28/03.

Test 11

Standard & Poor's Announces Change to U.S. Index

New York, NY, February 2, 2005 – Molson Coors Brewing Co. (NYSE:TAP) will replace Adolph Coors Co. (NYSE:RKY) in the S&P 500 after the close of trading on Tuesday, February 8. Adolph Coors is merging with S&P/TSX 60 constituent Molson Inc. in a deal expected to close on or about that date, pending final approval.

   Copyright © Standard & Poor's, a division of The McGraw-Hill Companies, Inc

Answer 11

Standard & Poor's Announces Change to U.S. Index

New York, NY, February 2, 2005 – <u>Molson Coors Brewing Co. (NYSE:TAP) will replace Adolph Coors Co. (NYSE:RKY) in the S&P 500</u> after the close of trading on Tuesday, February 8. <u>Adolph Coors (NYSE:RKY) is merging with Molson Inc.</u> in a deal expected to close on or about that date, pending final approval.

   Copyright © Standard & Poor's, a division of The McGraw-Hill Companies, Inc

Answer – There are no Tailwind stocks here. RKY is merging with Molson, Inc to form TAP. TAP will replace RKY in the S&P 500 Index, essentially replacing itself.

Test 12

LabOne Inc. Added to S&P SmallCap 600 Index

New York, NY, June 21, 2004 – LabOne Inc. (NASD:LABS) will replace New England Business Services (NYSE:NEB) in the S&P SmallCap 600 after the close of trading on Thursday, June 24, 2004. New England Business Services is being acquired by S&P 500 constituent Deluxe Corp. (NYSE:DLX) in a tender offer anticipated to be completed on or about that date.
    Copyright © Standard & Poor's, a division of The McGraw-Hill Companies, Inc

Answer 12

LabOne Inc. Added to S&P SmallCap 600 Index

New York, NY, June 21, 2004 – LabOne Inc. (NASD:LABS) will replace New England Business Services (NYSE:NEB) in the S&P SmallCap 600 after the close of trading on Thursday, June 24, 2004. New England Business Services is being acquired by S&P 500 constituent Deluxe Corp. (NYSE:DLX) in a tender offer anticipated to be completed on or about that date.
    Copyright © Standard & Poor's, a division of The McGraw-Hill Companies, Inc

Answer – LABS is a Tailwind stock. LABS will be added to the SmallCap 600 Index, replacing NEB. The date LABS will be added to the index is 6/24/04.

Chapter 7:   Trading The Tailwind Stocks

Now it is time to learn how to trade the Tailwind stocks. Each evening, or once a week, or once a month, you will check Standard and Poor's web site to see if there are any announced changes to their three main U.S. indexes, as detailed in **Chapter 5: Finding The Tailwind Stocks**. You will read the announcements and identify the Tailwind stocks, as detailed in **Chapter 5: Finding The Tailwind Stocks** and in **Chapter 6: Test Your Skills; Identify The Tailwind Stocks**. If you find a Tailwind stock, you will make note of the stock's ticker symbol and the effective date, as you did in **Chapter 6: Test Your Skills; Identify The Tailwind Stocks**. You will also need to make note of the closing price of the stock on the effective date. That price is an important part of the Tailwind Trading System, as you will learn in this chapter.

The procedures detailed in this chapter will take you step by step through the process of buying and selling the Tailwind stocks, so that you will be successful at making profits with these stocks. Section 1 provides details on finding the buy date and applying the filter. Section 2 details two main strategies that can be used to buy the Tailwind stocks. In Section 3,

you will learn how to set the price targets and sell the Tailwind stocks.
Section 4 provides guidance for setting limit orders and stop loss orders,
while Section 5 details the time frame for trading the Tailwind stocks.
Section 6 provides details on the money management component of the
Tailwind Trading System, and Section 7 provides variations that can be
used for the Tailwind Trading System.

1. Finding the Buy Date and Applying the Filter

First, let's review our proprietary Tailwind Sweet Spot formula. The
formula is:

Tailwind Sweet Spot = Event + Day + Filter.

Event = stock added to an S&P index.

Day = Day 56.

Filter = Filter A or Filter B.

You have already determined the Event has occurred and you have
recorded the necessary information; the ticker symbol, the effective date,

and the closing price of the stock on the effective date. The next step is determining the buy date, Day 56.

When a stock is added to an S&P index, it will be added to the index after the closing bell on the effective date that Standard and Poor's specifies in the announcement. You will begin counting forward from that day to find Day 56, which is the 56th business day after the effective date. <u>Do not</u> count the effective date. The first day to count, Day 1, will be the first business day after the effective date. Remember, a business day is a day when the stock market is open for business and stocks are traded. The days when the stock market is closed are not counted as business days, for example, weekends and some holidays. Count out to the 56th business day after the effective date, that day is the buy date. Write down that buy date.

If you are not sure which holidays that the stock market is closed, you can find that information at the New York Stock Exchange web site, http://www.nyse.com/about/newsevents/1176373643795.html, or at the NASDAQ web site, http://www.nasdaq.com/about/schedule.stm.

Now that you have the buy date, Day 56, the next step that you will need to do is apply the Filter, either Filter A or Filter B. You will apply the

Filter on Day 56. Do not forget to record the closing price of the stock on the effective date; you will need to use that price for the Filters. The difference between Filter A and Filter B is that Filter B does not require you to do a calculation to determine if the stock price has made it through the Filter, and Filter B will produce fewer stocks to trade than Filter A.

There is an important point to make here. Just before the buy date arrives for a stock, Day 56, check the news on the company and see if the company has been acquired by another company or has reached an agreement to be acquired by another company. The acquisition may be the result of a merger or a purchase. This can happen <u>between</u> the effective date and Day 56. If the stock has already been acquired by Day 56, then there is no stock to trade and it <u>is not</u> a candidate for the Tailwind Trading System and should be avoided. If there is an agreement to acquire the company, and the acquisition will take place after Day 56, then this stock <u>is not</u> a candidate for the Tailwind Trading System and should be avoided.

When the buy date arrives, Day 56, decide which Filter that you will use. Then, apply the Filter to the opening stock price to determine if it is a stock that you can trade using the Tailwind Trading System.

If the stock has undergone <u>a stock split between</u> the effective date and Day 56, you must take that into account when you apply the Filter. This adjustment is performed so the Filters can correctly compare the closing price of the stock on the effective date with the opening price of the stock on Day 56.

If the stock has undergone a 3 for 1 stock split, multiply the <u>opening</u> price of the stock on Day 56 by 3 before applying the Filter. If it was a 2 for 1 stock split, multiply the <u>opening</u> price of the stock on Day 56 by 2 before applying the Filter. If it was a 3 for 2 stock split, multiply the <u>opening</u> price of the stock on Day 56 by 1.5 before applying the Filter. If it was a 4 for 3 stock split, multiply the <u>opening</u> price of the stock on Day 56 by 1.33 before applying the Filter.

<u>Filter A:</u>

If you are using Filter A, the opening price of the stock on Day 56 <u>can not</u> be more than 4% above the closing price of the stock on the effective date. On Day 56, record the opening price of the stock. Then, determine if the opening price of the stock on Day 56 is more than 4% above the closing price of the stock on the effective date. If it is, then skip this stock, it should <u>not</u> be traded with the Tailwind Trading System. Use these steps to determine if the stock is more than 4% above the closing price of the stock on the effective date.

<u>Filter A:</u>

   Step 1: If the opening price of the stock on Day 56 <u>is equal to or less than</u> the closing price of the stock on the effective date, then the stock has made it through Filter A and it can be traded with the Tailwind Trading System, skip Step 2.

   Step 2: If the opening price of the stock on Day 56 <u>is greater than</u> the closing price of the stock on the effective date, then use this calculation to determine the difference between the two prices.

        (OP – CP) / CP = Difference

        OP = Opening price on Day 56.

        CP = Closing price on the effective date.

   Subtract the closing price of the stock on the effective date (CP) from the opening price of the stock on Day 56 (OP) and divide that result by the closing price of the stock on the effective date (CP).

If the Difference is 0.04 (4%) or less, then the stock has made it through Filter A and it can be traded with the Tailwind Trading System. If the Difference is 0.05 (5%) or more, then the stock has <u>not</u> made it through Filter A and it <u>should not</u> be traded with the Tailwind Trading System.

When performing this calculation, use only 2 decimal positions for the Difference. A Difference of 0.045 (4.5%) or greater would be rounded up to 0.05 (5%). A Difference of 0.044 (4.4%) or less would be rounded down to 0.04 (4%).

<u>Filter A Examples:</u>

OP = Opening price on Day 56.

CP = Closing price on the effective date.

1. Stock 1 -   CP is $47.35   OP is $44.71

The opening price of the stock on Day 56 is less than the closing price of the stock on the effective date. This stock has made it through Filter A and it can be traded with the Tailwind Trading System.

2. Stock 2 -   CP is $25.10   OP is $25.10

The opening price of the stock on Day 56 is equal to the closing price of the stock on the effective date. This stock has made it through Filter A and it can be traded with the Tailwind Trading System.

3. Stock 3 -   CP is $31.95   OP is $34.20

The opening price of the stock on Day 56 is greater than the closing price of the stock on the effective date.   Calculate the difference using the equation (OP – CP) / CP = Difference. Use only 2 decimal positions for the Difference.

      ($34.20 - $31.95) / $31.95 = 0.07

The opening price of the stock on Day 56 is 7% (0.07) higher than the closing price of the stock on the effective date. This stock has <u>not</u> made it through Filter A and it <u>should not</u> be traded with the Tailwind Trading System.

4. Stock 4 -   CP is $18.27   OP is $19.06

The opening price of the stock on Day 56 is greater than the closing price of the stock on the effective date.   Calculate the difference using the equation (OP – CP) / CP = Difference. Use only 2 decimal positions for the Difference.

$$(\$19.06 - \$18.27) / \$18.27 = 0.04$$

The opening price of the stock on Day 56 is 4% (0.04) higher than the closing price of the stock on the effective date. This stock has made it through Filter A and it can be traded with the Tailwind Trading System.

5. Stock 5 -   CP is $53.50   OP is $28.14   (the stock has undergone a 2 for 1 stock split between the effective date and Day 56).

First, take into account the stock split and multiply the opening price of the stock on Day 56 by 2 making that price $56.28. The opening price of the stock on Day 56 is greater than the closing price of the stock on the effective date.   Calculate the difference using the equation (OP – CP) / CP = Difference. Use only 2 decimal positions for the Difference.

$$(\$56.28 - \$53.50) / \$53.50 = 0.05$$

The opening price of the stock on Day 56 is 5% (0.05) higher than the closing price of the stock on the effective date. This stock has <u>not</u> made it through Filter A and it <u>should not</u> be traded with the Tailwind Trading System.

6. Stock 6 -   CP is $61.75   OP is $40.15   (the stock has undergone a 3 for 2 stock split between the effective date and Day 56).

First, take into account the stock split and multiply the opening price of the stock on Day 56 by 1.5 making that price $60.23. The opening price of the stock on Day 56 is less than the closing price of the stock on the effective date. This stock has made it through Filter A and it can be traded with the Tailwind Trading System.

Filter B:

If you are using Filter B, the opening price of the stock on Day 56 <u>must be</u> below the closing price of the stock on the effective date. On Day 56, record the opening price of the stock. Then, determine if the opening price of the stock on Day 56 is below the closing price of the stock on the effective date. If it is <u>not</u>, then skip this stock, it <u>should not</u> be traded with the Tailwind Trading System. Use these steps to determine if the stock is below the closing price of the stock on the effective date.

Filter B:

Step 1: If the opening price of the stock on Day 56 <u>is less than</u> the closing price of the stock on the effective date, then the stock has made it through Filter B and it can be traded with the Tailwind Trading System, skip Step 2.

Step 2: If the opening price of the stock on Day 56 <u>is equal to or greater than</u> the closing price of the stock on the effective date, then the stock has <u>not</u> made it through Filter B and it <u>should not</u> be traded with the Tailwind Trading System.

Filter B Examples:

OP = Opening price on Day 56.

CP = Closing price on the effective date.

1. Stock 1 -   CP is $47.35   OP is $44.71

The opening price of the stock on Day 56 is less than the closing price of the stock on the effective date. This stock has made it through Filter B and it can be traded with the Tailwind Trading System.

2. Stock 2 -   CP is $25.10   OP is $25.10

The opening price of the stock on Day 56 is equal to the closing price of the stock on the effective date.   This stock has <u>not</u> made it through Filter B and it <u>should not</u> be traded with the Tailwind Trading System.

3. Stock 3 -   CP is $31.95   OP is $34.20

The opening price of the stock on Day 56 is greater than the closing price of the stock on the effective date. This stock has <u>not</u> made it through Filter B and it <u>should not</u> be traded with the Tailwind Trading System.

4. Stock 4 -   CP is $53.50   OP is $28.14   (the stock has undergone a 2 for 1 stock split between the effective date and Day 56).

First, take into account the stock split and multiply the opening price of the stock on Day 56 by 2 making that price $56.28. The opening price of the stock on Day 56 is greater than the closing price of the stock on the effective date. This stock has <u>not</u> made it through Filter B and it <u>should not</u> be traded with the Tailwind Trading System.

5. Stock 5 -   CP is $61.75   OP is $40.15   (the stock has undergone a 3 for 2 stock split between the effective date and Day 56).

First, take into account the stock split and multiply the opening price of the stock on Day 56 by 1.5 making that price $60.23. The opening price of the stock on Day 56 is less than the closing price of the stock on the effective date. This stock has made it through Filter B and it can be traded with the Tailwind Trading System.

2. Buying the Tailwind Stocks

At this point you have determined that the Tailwind Event has occurred and you have found Day 56. Now, Day 56 has arrived and you have applied Filter A or Filter B, and the stock price has made it through the Filter.

Now it is time to buy the stock. The opening price of the Tailwind stock on Day 56 is the price that is used to track the performance of the Tailwind Trading System. This opening price is used because a fixed data point is needed in order to publish a track record like the Tailwind Trading System track record in **Chapter 10: Track Records and Statistics**.

There are two main strategies that can be used to buy the Tailwind stocks. <u>The first strategy</u> is to buy the stock on Day 56 as soon as you have determined that the stock price has passed through the filter that you have applied, either Filter A or Filter B. You want to buy the stock at a price that is close to the opening price on that day. Remember, the opening price of the stock on Day 56 is the price that is used to track the Tailwind Trading System. It is also the price that will be used to set the target price for selling the stock and making a profit. If you want to try and make your trading as mechanical as possible, then use this first strategy to buy the stock.

<u>The second strategy</u> that can be used to buy a Tailwind stock is to buy the stock sometime later in the day on Day 56 or sometime after Day 56. You may be able to buy the stock a few days after Day 56, or even a week or so after Day 56.

The advantage of this strategy is that you will know the opening price of the stock on Day 56 and you can use this strategy to try and buy the stock at a price that is lower than opening price of the stock on Day 56. The disadvantage of this strategy is that you may miss out on some trades.

The Tailwind Trading System is designed to make a 10% profit on a trade, as you will learn in section **3. Selling the Tailwind Stocks**. If you are going to use this second strategy to buy the Tailwind stock, either later in the day on Day 56 or sometime after that day, and the stock price reaches its 10% target price before you have been able to buy the stock, then do not buy the stock. You have missed this trade. As soon as the stock reaches its 10% target price, it is considered a winner and it is no longer tracked for the Tailwind Trading System track record. The stock price may drop from this point and may never reach the 10% target price again.

There is one more factor to consider if you are going to use this second strategy to buy the Tailwind stocks, either later in the day on Day 56 or sometime after Day 56. If the stock price has fallen 20% below the opening price of the stock on Day 56, before you have purchased the stock, then do not buy the stock. This stock is a loser. The Tailwind Trading System is designed to use a 20% stop loss, as you will learn in section **3. Selling the Tailwind Stocks**. As soon as the stock reaches its 20% stop loss price, it is considered a loser and it is no longer tracked for the Tailwind Trading System track record.

3. Selling the Tailwind Stocks

The Tailwind Trading System is designed to make a 10% profit on each trade. Stop losses are also used when trading the Tailwind stocks. By using stop losses, you will protect yourself from catastrophic losses, and you will know your profit potential and your risk potential before you enter a trade. A stop loss of 20% is used for each trade.

As mentioned earlier in this chapter, the opening price of the stock on Day 56 is the price that is used to track the performance of the Tailwind Trading System. It is also the price that will be used to set the target price and the stop loss price for selling the stock. The 10% target price is set at 10% above the opening price of the stock on Day 56 and the 20% stop loss price is set at 20% below the opening price of the stock on Day 56. Keep in mind that the 10% target price and the 20% stop loss price are not set based on the price that you paid for the stock. The target price and stop loss price are set based on the opening price of the stock on Day 56. The price that you paid for the stock may be higher or lower than the opening price of the stock on Day 56.

After you have purchased a Tailwind stock using one of the two main strategies described in section **2. Buying the Tailwind Stocks**, you then calculate the target price that you will sell the stock at. Take the opening

price of the stock on Day 56 and multiply that price by 10% (0.10). That will

give you the profit amount. Take that profit amount and add it to the

opening price of the stock on Day 56. That will give you the 10% target

price for selling the stock. That target price will be the 10% target price that

will be used to track the performance of the Tailwind Trading System. You

then place a limit order to sell your stock at that target price.

For example, let's say that First Example Inc., ticker symbol FEI, is

added to an S&P index. On Day 56, the opening price of the stock is

$31.50. Take that $31.50 price and multiply it by 0.10 and you get a profit

of three dollars and fifteen cents, $3.15. Take that profit of $3.15 and add it

to the opening price of the stock on Day 56, $31.50, and you get a target

price of $34.65. That target price of $34.65 will be the 10% target price that

will be used to track the performance of the Tailwind Trading System. You

then place a sell limit order to sell your shares of FEI at a price of $34.65.

When the stock reaches $34.65, your shares will be sold and you will make

your 10% profit.

You must also calculate the stop loss price for this trade. Take the

opening price of the stock on Day 56 and multiply that price by 20% (0.20).

That will give you the loss amount. Take that loss amount and subtract it from the opening price of the stock on Day 56. That will give you the stop loss price. That stop loss price will be the stop loss price that will be used to track the performance of the Tailwind Trading System. You then place a stop loss order to sell your stock if the stock price reaches that stop loss price.

To illustrate this, we will continue with our example, First Example Inc., ticker symbol FEI. The opening price of the stock on Day 56 is $31.50. Take that $31.50 price and multiply it by 0.20 and you get a value of six dollars and thirty cents, $6.30. Take that value of $6.30 and subtract it from the opening price of the stock on Day 56, $31.50, and you get a stop loss price of $25.20. That stop loss price of $25.20 will be the stop loss that will be used to track the performance of the Tailwind Trading System. You then place a stop loss order to sell your shares of FEI if the price reaches $25.20. If the stock reaches $25.20, your shares will be sold and you will have a loss of 20%.

There is an additional strategy that you can use to sell the Tailwind stocks. Do <u>not</u> place a sell limit order after you have purchased the stock; just place the stop loss order. Then, watch the stock to see if the price gets to the 10% target price or just above the 10% target price. Then, move your stop loss order below the current stock price in order to lock in that gain. If the stock price comes down and reaches the stop loss order, your order will be executed and the stock will be sold with your profit intact. On the other hand, if the stock continues to move higher, then you can move your stop loss higher as well and lock in more of a profit. Using this method to sell the stock would require more monitoring of the stock. If you are unable to watch the stock that closely, then use the sell limit order and the stop loss order to sell the stock as described in the example above.

4. Setting a Sell Limit Order and a Stop Loss Order

In section 3. Selling the Tailwind Stocks, you have learned that you will use a sell limit order and a stop loss order for each trade. There are a few ways that you can accomplish this. Some brokers allow you to place two orders on one stock. These are called OCO orders. OCO stands for One-Cancels-The-Other. With an OCO order, you can place a sell limit order to sell your shares of stock at the 10% target price and you can place a stop loss order to sell your shares of stock at the 20% stop loss price. If the sell limit order is executed, then the stop loss order is automatically canceled. If the stop loss order is executed, then the sell limit order is automatically canceled.

Some brokers offer similar types of orders known as conditional orders or bracketed orders. Check with your broker to see if they allow OCO orders, conditional orders, or bracketed orders.

You can also use a mental sell limit order or a mental stop loss order. For example, after you have purchased a Tailwind stock, you will have calculated the 10% target price and the 20% stop loss price. You can place a sell limit order to sell your shares of stock at the 10% target price. You would not place a physical order for the 20% stop loss. Watch the stock and if the stock price reaches the 20% stop loss price, you cancel the sell limit order and then sell the stock and take the loss.

You can also do this in reverse. You can place a stop loss order to sell your shares of stock if the stock price reaches the 20% stop loss price. You would not place a physical sell limit order for the 10% target price. Watch the stock and if the stock price reaches the 10% target price, you cancel the stop loss order and then sell the stock and take your profit.

5. Time Frame

Each Tailwind stock has 60 business days to reach its 10% target price. The <u>buy date is counted as the first business day</u> for the time frame, since the stock is purchased and tracked from the opening price on that day. Count out 60 business days from the buy date, that day is the sell date <u>if</u> <u>the target or stop loss is not reached before that day</u>. Write down that sell date.

If the Tailwind stock reaches its 10% target price before it reaches its 20% stop loss price or the sell date, then the trade is complete and it is counted as a winning trade. If the Tailwind stock reaches its 20% stop loss price before it reaches its 10% target price or the sell date, then the trade is complete and it is counted as a losing trade.

If the Tailwind stock does not reach its 10% target price or its 20% stop loss price by the sell date, then the stock should be sold and the trade closed out on the sell date. The closing price on the sell date is used in the Tailwind Trading System track record for trades that are closed out. This closing price is used because a fixed data point is needed in order to publish a track record like the Tailwind Trading System track record in **Chapter 10: Track Records and Statistics**. Also, this closing price will be compared to the opening price of the stock on the buy date to determine if it is a winning trade or a losing trade and the resulting profit or loss will be added to the total profit or loss listed in the overall track record.

6. Money Management

As with any stock trading or investing, you do not want to put all of your money into one trade. When trading stocks with the Tailwind Trading System, you will divide your money equally into 2, 3, or 4 trades. You will continue to keep your money divided as you complete trades and put that money into new trades, which will reinvest your profits and compound your money as you go along.

Before you begin using the Tailwind Trading System, decide how many trades you will divide your money into; 2, 3, or 4 trades. We ran computer simulations using up to 10 trades at a time. The computer simulations were performed using a cash account, not a margin account. Dividing the money equally into 2 trades produced the most profits. Dividing the money into 3 or 4 trades produced great results as well. Once the money is divided into 5 trades or more, the profits begin to move lower, the result of the law of diminishing returns. If the money is put into only one trade at a

89

time, then the trading will not be diversified and unnecessary risk is taken. The profits produced when using 2, 3, or 4 trades can be found in **Chapter 10: Track Records and Statistics**. You can use the data, and your own risk tolerance and trading style, to decide how you would like to divide your money. While dividing the money into 2 trades may have produced more profits, you may feel that 3 or 4 trades may be safer for you.

Once you have divided your money into equal amounts, when you find a stock to trade with the Tailwind Trading System, enter the trade with one of your amounts of money. You will put the rest of the money into trades when you find more stocks to trade with the Tailwind Trading System. If you have divided your money into 2 trades, then you will be involved in a maximum of 2 trades at any given time. If you have divided your money into 3 trades, then you will be involved in a maximum of 3 trades at any given time. If you have divided your money into 4 trades, then you will be involved in a maximum of 4 trades at any given time.

When a trade is completed, either by the stock reaching its target price, or the stock hitting its stop loss price, or the trade being closed out at the end of the 60 day time frame, you take that money and add it back into what ever amount of money that you have in cash and then rebalance the amounts into equal sums. You will put the money into the next trades that you find with the Tailwind Trading System.

There will be times when you will have your money in only 1 active trade and there will be times when you may have your money in the maximum number of active trades, 2, 3 or 4, depending on how you chose to divide your money. If you have your money in only 1 active trade, you will have the rest of your money available in cash to put into other trades when you find them with the Tailwind Trading System. Think of your brokerage account as having two sections where your money will be. One section will be the current trades that you have put money into; the other section will be the remaining amounts of cash waiting for the next trades that you find with the Tailwind Trading System. For example, you may have decided to divide your money into 3 trades. You have one amount of money currently in a trade, so you keep your other two amounts of money in cash waiting for the next trades that you find with the Tailwind Trading System. When you find a trade, you then take one of the amounts of money that you have in cash and put it into the trade.

Try to keep your money split into equal amounts, or as close to equal amounts as you can make it. As trades are completed, you will have to rebalance your amounts of money based on the amount of money you have been making or losing on trades, how many trades you have decided to divide your money into, and how many amounts of money are currently in trades and how many amounts of money are currently in cash.

Let's use an example to show how the money management system works in the Tailwind Trading System. Commissions and dividends are not included in this example. We will begin with $10,000.00 in our brokerage account. We will use a cash account, not a margin account. We have decided to divide the money equally into 4 trades. This means that we will be involved with a maximum of 4 trades at any given time.

First, we divide the money into 4 equal amounts of $2,500.00. These 4 amounts of money are sitting in cash, waiting for trades that we find with the Tailwind Trading System. You do not actually physically separate your amounts of money in your brokerage account; you will keep track of your amounts of money on paper or in a spreadsheet. To help keep track of your amounts of money, label them as Part A, Part B, Part C, and Part D. You will use Part A and Part B, or Part A, Part B, and Part C, or Part A, Part B, Part C, and Part D depending on the number of trades you have decided to divide your money into.

For our example, we have divided our money into 4 amounts. We will label our 4 amounts of money as Part A, Part B, Part C, and Part D. Then we will look for stocks to trade using the Tailwind Trading System.

Let's say that we find 2 stocks to trade. We put one amount of money, Part A - $2,500.00, into one trade and we put another amount of money, Part B - $2,500.00, into the other trade. We still have 2 amounts of money in cash, each $2,500.00. They are Part C and Part D.

Let's say that the trade that Part A is in hits its target price. It has made a 10% profit. Part A is now $2,750.00, the original $2,500.00 plus the 10% profit, $250.00. We add this money to the money that is in cash, Part C and Part D. Now we have a total of $7,750.00 sitting in cash, consisting of Part A = $2,750.00, Part C = $2,500.00, and Part D = $2,500.00. The other amount of money, Part B, is still in a trade. Now, since the trade that Part A was involved in is complete, we take the total amount of money that we have in cash and rebalance it into equal parts as best as possible.

We have $7,750.00 sitting in cash. Before we began trading, we decided that we will divide the money into 4 trades. One part, Part B, is still in a trade so we leave that amount of money alone. That leaves us with three available parts still sitting in cash, Part A, Part C, and Part D. Now we take the $7,750.00 that is sitting in cash and rebalance it for the three available parts. We take $7,750.00 and divide by 3 and that gives us $2,583.00 plus a remainder. Now we divide it as best we can and put $2,583.00 into Part A, $2,583.00 into Part C, and $2,584.00 into Part D, that gives us the total of $7,750.00. You will not always be able to divide the money into precisely equal parts and you will not always be able to put the exact amount from a part into a trade, just do the best that you can.

Now, let's say that two more trades come along. We still have Part B, $2,500.00, in one of our original trades, so we have Part A, Part C, and Part D available in cash. We put Part A, $2,583.00, into one trade and Part C, $2,583.00, into the other trade. So now we have only Part D, $2,584.00, in cash.

Now, let's say that the trade that Part B is in is completed. Part B had $2,500.00 in the trade. It is a losing trade; it hit its stop loss and loses 20% or $500.00. What we have left from Part B is now $2,000.00 ($2,500.00 - $500.00). Since the trade that Part B was involved in is complete, we add this money to the money that we have in cash and we then take the total amount of money that we have in cash and rebalance it into equal parts as best as possible.

We now have $4,584.00 sitting in cash. That is from Part B, $2,000.00 and Part D, $2,584.00. We take that $4,584.00 and divide it between the 2 available parts still sitting in cash, which would be Part B and Part D. Part A and Part C are not available, they are currently in trades. So we take the $4,584.00 and divide by 2 and that gives us $2,292.00. Now we put $2,292.00 into Part B and $2,292.00 onto Part D and wait for the next trades to come along.

That is how the money management system works in the Tailwind Trading System. As trades are completed, you will continue to rebalance your amounts of money based on the amount of money you currently have in cash and the total number of available parts that you have in cash. By continuing to add the profits into new trades, the total amount of money will continue to compound as time goes on.

The examples that we just went through are the same technique that we used when we ran the computer simulations. Also, the computer simulations purchased the stocks at the open price on Day 56, which is the first strategy for purchasing the stocks as described in section **2. Buying the Tailwind Stocks**. You can see the results in **Chapter 10: Track Records and Statistics**. You will see in the results when using Filter A and 2 trades, a portfolio that began with $100,000 in 2000 became more than $800,000 after 2008.

There is another important point to make here. When you complete a trade and put the money back into your cash account, ready for trading, wait for the next "new" trade to come along and put the money into that trade. Do not put the money into a trade that may have started 10 days ago, but your money was tied up at that time in other trades. Wait for the next new trade opportunity and buy on Day 56. We ran the computer simulations in that manner.

For example, let's say that we have our money divided into 4 trades, Part A, Part B, Part C, and Part D. All 4 of our amounts of money are currently involved in trades; we have no amounts of money in cash. On June 1st, a new trade comes along but we do not have any amounts of money available so we let it pass by. On June 15th, the trade that Part A was involved in is complete. We do not put that money into the missed trade from June 1st. We put that money into cash and wait for the next new trade. On June 27th, a new trade comes along. June 27th is Day 56 for this trade. We have one available amount of money, Part A, so we put that amount of money into this new trade on June 27th. This scenario will occur often. You will not trade all of the picks that the Tailwind Trading System generates. Only a portion of the total amount of picks was traded when the computer simulations were run and the results were outstanding, as you will see in **Chapter 10: Track Records and Statistics**. As we mentioned earlier in this chapter, once you begin dividing your money into 5 or more parts, the law of diminishing returns begins to take effect.

Another point to make here is that you can always change the number of trades that you have divided your money into. For example, let's say that when you began using the Tailwind Trading System, you decided to divide your money into 4 trades. You have Part A, Part B, Part C, and Part D. At some point in the future, you decide that you want to divide your money into only 3 trades instead of 4 trades. All you need to do then is eliminate Part D and rebalance your money accordingly and just use Part A, Part B, and Part C from that point forward. You can also do the same thing in the other direction. If you started by using 2 trades, Part A and Part B, and now you want to use 3 trades, just add Part C, rebalance your money accordingly and use Part A, Part B, and Part C from that point forward.

7. Variations for the Tailwind Trading System

There are several variations that you can use for the Tailwind Trading System. Instead of using a 20% stop loss on a Tailwind trade, you can use a 30% stop loss. This produces a winning percentage that is a few percentage points higher than with the 20% stop loss, however, you would lose more money on a losing trade.

You would use a 10% profit target and a 30% stop loss. Follow the guidelines in section 3. Selling the Tailwind Stocks and replace the 20% stop loss with a 30% stop loss.

Another variation that you can use is a 90 day time frame instead of a 60 day time frame. This produces a winning percentage that is a few percentage points higher than with the 60 day time frame, however, you may be holding a trade for a longer period of time. This longer time frame may be useful for someone who is away on business often and does not have the time or the access to monitor the trades on a daily or weekly basis. Follow the guidelines in section 5. Time Frame and replace the 60 day time frame with a 90 day time frame.

The data for all of these variations can be found in **Chapter 10: Track Records and Statistics**. You can use the data to decide if you would like to use any of the variations.

To review, you can use the main parameters:

1) Filter A, 10% profit, 20% stop loss, and a 60 day time frame.

2) Filter B, 10% profit, 20% stop loss, and a 60 day time frame.

or the variations:

3) Filter A, 10% profit, 20% stop loss, and a 90 day time frame.

4) Filter B, 10% profit, 20% stop loss, and a 90 day time frame.

5) Filter A, 10% profit, 30% stop loss, and a 60 day time frame.

6) Filter B, 10% profit, 30% stop loss, and a 60 day time frame.

7) Filter A, 10% profit, 30% stop loss, and a 90 day time frame.

8) Filter B, 10% profit, 30% stop loss, and a 90 day time frame.

Chapter 8:   Tailwind Trading Guidelines

Our Tailwind Trading Guidelines summarize what you have learned in the previous chapters. For further details about any information in the Tailwind Trading Guidelines, refer to that chapter.

1. Decide how many trades that you want to divide your money into. You can divide your money into 2, 3, or 4 trades.

2. Check Standard & Poor's web site on a regular basis to find the announcements of changes to their main U.S indexes; the S&P 500 Index, the MidCap 400 Index, and the SmallCap 600 Index. You can choose to check the web site each evening, or once a week, or once a month.

3. Read the announcements and identify the Tailwind stocks. Look for stocks that are <u>added</u> to an index, including stocks that are transferring from a smaller index to a larger index. Look for these phrases or similar phrases: "add", "added", "replace", "transfer".

4. Avoid stocks that are added to an index when the stock to be added is:

   A) Transferring from a larger index to a smaller index.

   B) The result of a merger, when the "new" company replaces the "old" company in the same index.

   C) The result of an acquisition, when the "new" company replaces the acquired company in the same index.

   D) The result of a spin-off.

   E) Added on a date "to be announced".

   F) Added on a date that is more than seven business day after the announcement.

5. When you find a Tailwind stock, write down the ticker symbol of the stock, the effective date, and the closing price of the stock on the effective date.

6. Occasionally, sometime after the initial announcement has been made, Standard & Poor's will change the effective date. Watch for any date changes and keep track of the new effective date.

7. Use the Tailwind Sweet Spot formula.

Tailwind Sweet Spot = Event + Day + Filter

8. You have completed steps 2 through 6 and have found a Tailwind stock. This is the Tailwind Event in the Tailwind Sweet Spot formula. Proceed to step 9 to find the Day in the Tailwind Sweet Spot formula.

9. Day 56 is the Day in the Tailwind Sweet Spot formula. Count out 56 business days from the effective date. This will be the buy date. Write down that date. <u>Do not</u> count the effective date. The first day to count, Day 1, will be the first business day after the effective date. A business day is a day when the stock market is open for business and stocks are traded. The days when the stock market is closed are not counted as business days, for example, weekends and some holidays.

10. Just before the buy date arrives for a stock, Day 56, check the news on the company and see if the company has been acquired by another company or has reached an agreement to be acquired by another company. The acquisition may be the result of a merger or a purchase.

Avoid stocks that have already been acquired by Day 56, or have reached an agreement by Day 56 to be acquired and the acquisition will occur after Day 56.

11. When Day 56 has arrived; apply Filter A or Filter B to the opening price of the stock. If the stock has undergone a stock split between the effective date and Day 56, take that into account when you apply the Filter.

12. When using Filter A, the opening price of the stock on Day 56 can not be more than 4% above the closing price of the stock on the effective date. When calculating the difference between the two prices, use only 2 decimal positions. Round up or down as needed.

13. When using Filter B, the opening stock price on Day 56 must be below the closing price of the stock on the effective date.

14. If the stock price has made it through Filter A or Filter B, then it is a Tailwind stock and can be purchased and you can proceed to the next

103

step. If the stock price has not made it through Filter A or Filter B, then stop here.

15. You can use two strategies to buy the stock. <u>The first strategy</u> is to buy the stock on Day 56 as soon as you have determined that the stock price has passed through the filter that you have applied, either Filter A or Filter B. You want to buy the stock at a price that is close to the opening price on that day. The opening price of the stock on Day 56 is the price that is used to track the Tailwind Trading System. It is also the price that will be used to set the target price and the stop loss price.

16. <u>The second strategy</u> that can be used to buy a Tailwind stock is to buy the stock sometime later in the day on Day 56 or sometime after Day 56. The advantage of this strategy is that you will know the opening price of the stock on Day 56 and you can use this strategy to try and buy the stock at a price that is lower than opening price of the stock on Day 56. If you are using this buying strategy and the stock price reaches its 10% target price or its 20% stop loss price before you have purchased the stock, then do not buy the stock. You have missed this trade.

17. After you have purchased the stock, calculate the target price and stop loss price. The 10% target price is set at 10% <u>above</u> the opening price of the stock on Day 56 and the 20% stop loss price is set at 20% <u>below</u> the opening price of the stock on Day 56. Keep in mind that the 10% target price and the 20% stop loss price are not set based on the price that you paid for the stock. The target price and stop loss price are set based on the opening price of the stock on Day 56. The price that you paid for the stock may be higher or lower than the opening price of the stock on Day 56.

18. Place a sell limit order at the target price and place a stop loss order at the stop loss price.

19. Set the time frame at 60 business days. The <u>buy date is counted as the first business day</u> for the time frame, since the stock is tracked from the opening price on that day. Count out 60 business days from the buy date, that day is the sell date <u>if the target or stop loss is not reached before that day</u>. Write down that sell date.

20. If the Tailwind stock reaches its 10% target price before it reaches its 20% stop loss price or the sell date, then the trade is complete and it is counted as a winning trade. If the Tailwind stock reaches its 20% stop loss price before it reaches its 10% target price or the sell date, then the trade is complete and it is counted as a losing trade. If the Tailwind stock does not reach its 10% target price or its 20% stop loss price by the sell date, then the stock should be sold and the trade closed out. The closing price on the sell date is used in the Tailwind Trading System track record for trades that are closed out. That price will be compared to the opening price of the stock on the buy date to determine if it is a winning trade or a losing trade.

21. When a trade is completed, rebalance your amounts of money based on the total amount of money you currently have in cash and the total number of available parts that you have in cash.

Chapter 9:   References

1. *S&P U.S. Indices Index Methodology*

   September, 2007

   Standard & Poor's

   www.standardandpoors.com

Chapter 10:   Track Records and Statistics

This chapter contains the overall track records and the detailed track record for the Tailwind Trading System. The first overall track records included in this chapter show the results when using the main parameters; a 10% profit, 20% stop loss, 60 day time frame, and Filter A or Filter B.

The detailed track record included at the end of this chapter shows the results when using one of the main parameters; a 10% profit, 20% stop loss, 60 day time frame, and Filter A.

The overall track records using the variation parameters are also included in this chapter.

Included in all of the overall track records are the results when 2 trades, 3 trades, or 4 trades were used. These are the computer simulated results using the money management component of the Tailwind Trading System that is described in **Chapter 7: Trading The Tailwind Stocks**, section "6. Money Management".

Also included in this chapter is a comparison of the Tailwind Trading System performance against stock market benchmarks, as well as additional statistics about the number of target prices that are hit in one business day, five business days, and fifteen business days. These statistics, along with the overall track records and the detailed track record, may help you decide which buy and sell strategies and parameters that you may want to use for trading the Tailwind stocks.

The overall track records for the Tailwind Trading System using the main parameters are shown in Section 1. Section 2 shows a comparison of the Tailwind Trading System performance against stock market benchmarks. The overall track records using the variation parameters are shown in Section 3, followed by the additional statistics in Section 4, Section 5, and Section 6. The detailed track record is then listed for the Tailwind Trading System in Section 7.

1. Overall Track Records

The tables shown below contain the overall track records for the Tailwind Trading System. <u>Both tables show the results using Day 56 as the buy day, a profit target of 10%, a stop loss of 20%, and a time frame of 60 days</u>. One table shows the results using <u>Filter A</u> and the other table shows the results using <u>Filter B</u>. Commissions and dividends are not included in the calculations.

If a stock did not reach its target price or its stop loss price in the specified time frame, it is counted as a winning trade or a losing trade, determined by using the difference of the opening price on the buy day and the closing price on the sell date. The resulting profit or loss has been added to the total profit or loss listed in the overall track records. This is described in **Chapter 7: Trading The Tailwind Stocks**, section "5. Time Frame". You will see this in detail when you look through the detailed track record at the end of this chapter.

There are a few notes to point out here. When a stock was closed out and the profit or loss was zero, it was counted as a losing trade. Also, the stocks have been separated by year based on the date the stock was added to an S&P index. That is when the Tailwind "stock pick" was made. For example, a stock may have been added to an S&P index on December 10th, 2000. That stock is counted in the year 2000 in the overall track records and the detailed track record, even though the buy date, Day 56, would occur sometime in 2001. You will see this when you look through the detailed track record at the end of this chapter.

Also, there is one Tailwind stock from 2000 and one Tailwind stock from 2001 that are not included in the overall track records or the detailed track record. These companies were either acquired by another company or went out of business, and historical stock quote data was not available for them. We will attempt to include them in a future release.

Also, there are two Tailwind stocks from 2008 that are not included in the overall track records or the detailed track record because they did not hit their target price, stop loss price or close out date at the time of publication. We will include them in the next edition.

In addition, two or three Tailwind stocks from 2008 are not counted in the overall track records when the time frame was 90 days because these stocks did not hit their target price, stop loss price or close out date at the time of publication. As a result, you will see in the overall track records that the total picks in 2008 in the 90 day time frame tables do not match the corresponding 60 day time frame table. We will include them in the next edition.

The first table listed here shows the results when using Filter A and the second table shows the results when using Filter B. A starting amount of $100,000 was used to begin the portfolios. <u>You will see in the first table, using Filter A and 2 trades, the portfolio grew to more than $850,000 dollars.</u>

Of course, not everyone has a portfolio of $100,000. We ran the computer simulations with various amounts used as the beginning portfolio. Using Filter A and 2 trades, a beginning portfolio of $5,000 grew to more than $40,000, a beginning portfolio of $10,000 grew to more than $85,000 and a beginning portfolio of $20,000 grew to more than $170,000. This data is not shown in the tables listed in this chapter.

Also, the total number of trades that the computer simulations performed to produce the results shown in the tables was as follows: in the first table, using Filter A, 158 trades when using "2 trades", 229 trades when using "3 trades", and 294 trades when using "4 trades". In the second table, using Filter B, 155 trades when using "2 trades", 220 trades when using "3 trades", and 276 trades when using "4 trades".

In the detailed track record that is located at the end of this chapter, you will find the details about all of the stocks in the first table listed here, using Filter A, a 10% target, 20% stop loss, and a 60 day time frame.

The keys to reading the columns of the tables are as follows:

YEAR – the year that is used to catalog and track the stocks for the overall track records.

PICKS - the total number of picks.

WIN - the number of winning trades.

LOSE - the number of losing trades.

RATE - the winning percentage.

PROFIT - this is the total profit from adding up the profits and losses from all of the winning trades and the losing trades.

2 TRADES, 3 TRADES, 4 TRADES – this shows the results of our computer trading simulation using 2 trades, 3 trades, or 4 trades. The portfolio began with $100,000.

PORTFOLIO – this shows the balance in the portfolio at the end of each year. The portfolio began with $100,000.

GAIN - the percentage of gain or loss from the prior year's portfolio balance. For the first year, this would be the gain or loss from the initial portfolio balance of $100,000.

Tailwind Trading System

Chapter 10: Track Records and Statistics

A) Parameters =   Filter: A   Target price: 10%   Stop loss price: 20%   Time frame: 60 business days

YEAR	PICKS	WIN	LOSE	RATE	PROFIT	2 TRADES		3 TRADES		4 TRADES	
						PORTFOLIO	GAIN	PORTFOLIO	GAIN	PORTFOLIO	GAIN
2000	154	106	48	69%	101%	$169,207.00	69%	$185,211.00	85%	$157,684.00	58%
2001	81	60	21	74%	215%	$286,316.00	69%	$297,732.00	61%	$230,002.00	46%
2002	47	30	17	64%	49%	$264,627.00	-8%	$285,088.00	-4%	$228,888.00	0%
2003	28	20	8	71%	112%	$310,121.00	17%	$314,860.00	10%	$264,687.00	16%
2004	47	35	12	74%	141%	$453,122.00	46%	$431,240.00	37%	$347,305.00	31%
2005	45	31	14	69%	121%	$604,554.00	33%	$508,214.00	18%	$391,355.00	13%
2006	53	40	13	75%	162%	$843,990.00	40%	$607,075.00	19%	$474,605.00	21%
2007	77	43	34	56%	-54%	$675,918.00	-20%	$538,669.00	-11%	$460,914.00	-3%
2008	95	59	36	62%	-108%	$856,529.00	27%	$424,274.00	-21%	$342,170.00	-26%
TOTALS:	627	424	203	68%	739%	TOTAL:	273%	TOTAL:	194%	TOTAL:	156%

B) Parameters =   Filter: B   Target price: 10%   Stop loss price: 20%   Time frame: 60 business days

YEAR	PICKS	WIN	LOSE	RATE	PROFIT	2 TRADES		3 TRADES		4 TRADES	
						PORTFOLIO	GAIN	PORTFOLIO	GAIN	PORTFOLIO	GAIN
2000	139	96	43	69%	101%	$99,993.00	0%	$125,728.00	26%	$131,481.00	31%
2001	65	45	20	69%	93%	$129,733.00	30%	$175,360.00	39%	$182,340.00	39%
2002	43	28	15	65%	69%	$141,421.00	9%	$170,298.00	-3%	$187,843.00	3%
2003	22	16	6	73%	81%	$169,558.00	20%	$192,943.00	13%	$207,122.00	10%
2004	40	29	11	73%	109%	$193,835.00	14%	$239,468.00	24%	$256,629.00	24%
2005	38	27	11	71%	93%	$222,543.00	15%	$273,668.00	14%	$263,919.00	3%
2006	39	30	9	77%	110%	$326,167.00	47%	$379,226.00	39%	$343,982.00	30%
2007	65	38	27	58%	-7%	$290,825.00	-11%	$330,671.00	-13%	$316,694.00	-8%
2008	86	54	32	63%	-69%	$376,390.00	29%	$261,057.00	-21%	$254,573.00	-20%
TOTALS:	537	363	174	68%	580%	TOTAL:	153%	TOTAL:	118%	TOTAL:	112%

114

2. Comparison to Market Benchmarks

This chart shows how the Tailwind Trading System performed against two well known stock market benchmarks, the S&P 500 Index and the Dow Jones Industrial Average. The results for the Tailwind Trading System are from one of the tables above; table A in Section 1, from the portfolio using 2 trades. Commissions and dividends are not included in calculating the returns for the Tailwind Trading System, the S&P 500, or the Dow. The Tailwind Trading System out performed in 7 out of 9 years, missing only in 2003 and 2007.

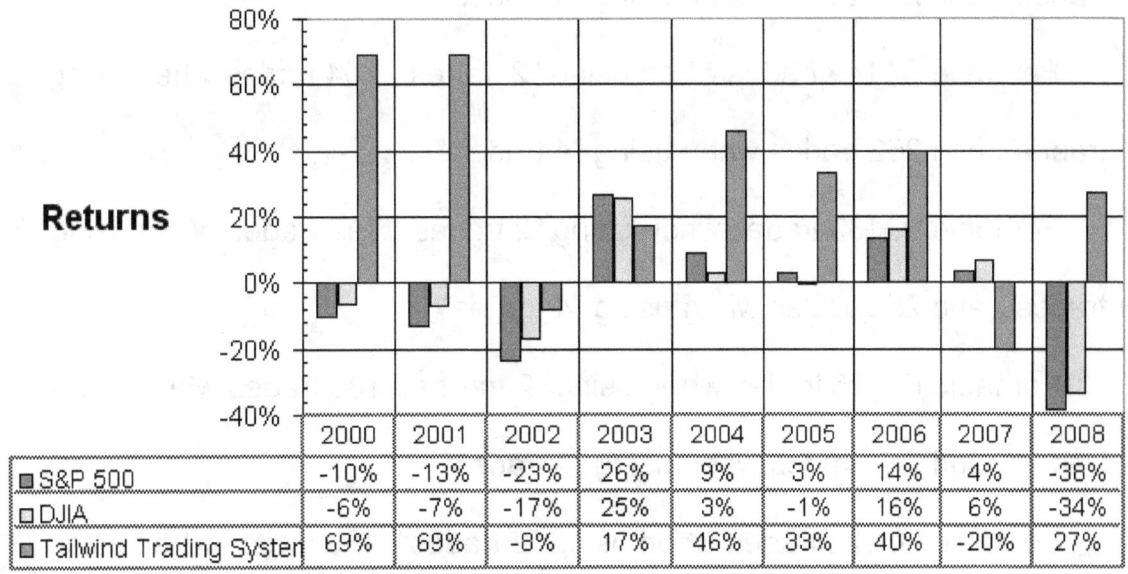

Year	2000	2001	2002	2003	2004	2005	2006	2007	2008
S&P 500	-10%	-13%	-23%	26%	9%	3%	14%	4%	-38%
DJIA	-6%	-7%	-17%	25%	3%	-1%	16%	6%	-34%
Tailwind Trading System	69%	69%	-8%	17%	46%	33%	40%	-20%	27%

Year

S&P 500   DJIA   Tailwind Trading System

3. Overall Track Records – Variations

The tables shown below contain the overall track records for the Tailwind Trading System using the variation parameters that are discussed in **Chapter 7: Trading The Tailwind Stocks**, section "8. Variations for the Tailwind Trading System". <u>All of the tables show the results using Day 56 as the buy day.</u>

The total number of trades that the computer simulations performed to produce the results shown in the tables was as follows:

For table C, 154 trades when using "2 trades", 222 trades when using "3 trades", and 278 trades when using "4 trades".

For table D, 149 trades when using "2 trades", 204 trades when using "3 trades", and 262 trades when using "4 trades".

For table E, 133 trades when using "2 trades", 197 trades when using "3 trades", and 256 trades when using "4 trades".

For table F, 125 trades when using "2 trades", 186 trades when using "3 trades", and 241 trades when using "4 trades".

For table G, 128 trades when using "2 trades", 189 trades when using "3 trades", and 234 trades when using "4 trades".

For table H, 113 trades when using "2 trades", 176 trades when using "3 trades", and 222 trades when using "4 trades".

The keys to reading the columns of the tables are as follows:

YEAR – the year that is used to catalog and track the stocks for the overall track records.

PICKS - the total number of picks.

WIN - the number of winning trades.

LOSE - the number of losing trades.

RATE - the winning percentage.

PROFIT - this is the total profit from adding up the profits and losses from all of the winning trades and the losing trades.

2 TRADES, 3 TRADES, 4 TRADES – this shows the results of our computer trading simulation using 2 trades, 3 trades, or 4 trades. The portfolio began with $100,000.

PORTFOLIO – this shows the balance in the portfolio at the end of each year. The portfolio began with $100,000.

GAIN - the percentage of gain or loss from the prior year's portfolio balance. For the first year, this would be the gain or loss from the initial portfolio balance of $100,000.

Tailwind Trading System

Chapter 10: Track Records and Statistics

C) Parameters = Filter: A   Target price: 10%   Stop loss price: 20%   Time frame: 90 business days

YEAR	PICKS	WIN	LOSE	RATE	PROFIT	2 TRADES		3 TRADES		4 TRADES	
						PORTFOLIO	GAIN	PORTFOLIO	GAIN	PORTFOLIO	GAIN
2000	154	107	47	69%	126%	$145,374.00	45%	$166,566.00	67%	$145,263.00	45%
2001	81	60	21	74%	206%	$243,425.00	67%	$265,636.00	59%	$210,692.00	45%
2002	47	30	17	64%	41%	$290,679.00	19%	$270,845.00	2%	$197,350.00	-6%
2003	28	22	6	79%	118%	$318,835.00	10%	$298,824.00	10%	$231,011.00	17%
2004	47	37	10	79%	205%	$419,747.00	32%	$412,981.00	38%	$332,526.00	44%
2005	45	32	13	71%	120%	$539,716.00	29%	$522,594.00	27%	$394,190.00	19%
2006	53	42	11	79%	219%	$731,656.00	36%	$706,209.00	35%	$527,587.00	34%
2007	77	49	28	64%	-27%	$692,181.00	-5%	$755,444.00	7%	$577,875.00	10%
2008	93	59	34	63%	-90%	$879,765.00	27%	$549,775.00	-27%	$427,980.00	-26%
TOTALS:	625	438	187	70%	918%	TOTAL:	260%	TOTAL:	218%	TOTAL:	182%

D) Parameters = Filter: B   Target price: 10%   Stop loss price: 20%   Time frame: 90 business days

YEAR	PICKS	WIN	LOSE	RATE	PROFIT	2 TRADES		3 TRADES		4 TRADES	
						PORTFOLIO	GAIN	PORTFOLIO	GAIN	PORTFOLIO	GAIN
2000	139	97	42	70%	126%	$136,441.00	36%	$151,145.00	51%	$144,194.00	44%
2001	65	45	20	69%	85%	$170,899.00	25%	$205,713.00	36%	$196,272.00	36%
2002	43	28	15	65%	61%	$190,753.00	12%	$235,170.00	14%	$199,330.00	2%
2003	22	17	5	77%	79%	$201,324.00	6%	$255,953.00	9%	$229,294.00	15%
2004	40	31	9	78%	165%	$251,582.00	25%	$326,918.00	28%	$281,714.00	23%
2005	38	27	11	71%	95%	$253,773.00	1%	$364,032.00	11%	$305,785.00	9%
2006	39	31	8	79%	155%	$369,397.00	46%	$526,896.00	45%	$434,300.00	42%
2007	65	43	22	66%	19%	$371,330.00	1%	$472,689.00	-10%	$465,471.00	7%
2008	84	54	30	64%	-60%	$431,983.00	16%	$403,698.00	-15%	$396,907.00	-15%
TOTALS:	535	373	162	70%	725%	TOTAL:	168%	TOTAL:	169%	TOTAL:	163%

118

Chapter 10: Track Records and Statistics

E) Parameters = Filter: A   Target price: 10%   Stop loss price: 30%   Time frame: 60 business days

YEAR	PICKS	WIN	LOSE	RATE	PROFIT	2 TRADES		3 TRADES		4 TRADES	
						PORTFOLIO	GAIN	PORTFOLIO	GAIN	PORTFOLIO	GAIN
2000	154	119	34	77%	208%	$121,694.00	22%	$144,257.00	44%	$122,727.00	23%
2001	81	63	18	78%	251%	$203,921.00	68%	$230,699.00	60%	$181,909.00	48%
2002	47	31	16	66%	53%	$198,126.00	-3%	$200,940.00	-13%	$192,953.00	6%
2003	28	21	7	75%	142%	$232,186.00	17%	$244,119.00	21%	$239,949.00	24%
2004	47	36	11	77%	161%	$339,248.00	46%	$321,058.00	32%	$328,639.00	37%
2005	45	31	14	69%	147%	$471,926.00	39%	$409,806.00	28%	$383,754.00	17%
2006	53	42	11	79%	217%	$705,251.00	49%	$520,187.00	27%	$471,098.00	23%
2007	77	43	34	56%	-91%	$607,472.00	-14%	$469,133.00	-10%	$415,588.00	-12%
2008	95	66	29	69%	-123%	$437,196.00	-28%	$325,311.00	-31%	$271,926.00	-35%
TOTALS:	627	452	174	72%	965%	TOTAL:	196%	TOTAL:	158%	TOTAL:	131%

F) Parameters = Filter: B   Target price: 10%   Stop loss price: 30%   Time frame: 60 business days

YEAR	PICKS	WIN	LOSE	RATE	PROFIT	2 TRADES		3 TRADES		4 TRADES	
						PORTFOLIO	GAIN	PORTFOLIO	GAIN	PORTFOLIO	GAIN
2000	139	108	31	78%	207%	$84,387.00	-16%	$122,187.00	22%	$126,902.00	27%
2001	65	48	17	74%	139%	$112,675.00	34%	$157,298.00	29%	$162,960.00	28%
2002	43	29	14	67%	93%	$131,896.00	17%	$159,007.00	1%	$179,228.00	10%
2003	22	17	5	77%	111%	$158,137.00	20%	$198,170.00	25%	$212,521.00	19%
2004	40	30	10	75%	139%	$203,246.00	29%	$284,494.00	44%	$293,638.00	38%
2005	38	27	11	71%	119%	$283,214.00	39%	$315,064.00	11%	$323,482.00	10%
2006	39	32	7	82%	164%	$423,857.00	50%	$445,250.00	41%	$403,424.00	25%
2007	65	38	27	58%	-48%	$310,621.00	-27%	$330,920.00	-26%	$348,245.00	-14%
2008	86	61	25	71%	-68%	$255,806.00	-18%	$224,909.00	-32%	$268,658.00	-23%
TOTALS:	537	390	147	73%	856%	TOTAL:	128%	TOTAL:	115%	TOTAL:	120%

Tailwind Trading System

Chapter 10: Track Records and Statistics

G) Parameters = Filter: A   Target price: 10%   Stop loss price: 30%   Time frame: 90 business days

YEAR	PICKS	WIN	LOSE	RATE	PROFIT	2 TRADES		3 TRADES		4 TRADES	
						PORTFOLIO	GAIN	PORTFOLIO	GAIN	PORTFOLIO	GAIN
2000	154	120	34	78%	238%	$140,289.00	40%	$154,507.00	55%	$128,405.00	28%
2001	81	65	16	80%	263%	$275,960.00	97%	$219,087.00	42%	$194,164.00	51%
2002	47	32	15	68%	40%	$292,251.00	6%	$220,986.00	1%	$188,814.00	-3%
2003	28	23	5	82%	154%	$301,641.00	3%	$258,034.00	17%	$224,526.00	19%
2004	47	39	8	83%	233%	$352,345.00	17%	$321,787.00	25%	$308,700.00	37%
2005	45	33	12	73%	133%	$501,349.00	42%	$473,587.00	47%	$393,908.00	28%
2006	53	45	8	85%	291%	$722,941.00	44%	$619,111.00	31%	$546,865.00	39%
2007	77	50	27	65%	-97%	$738,560.00	2%	$585,376.00	-5%	$500,759.00	-8%
2008	92	66	26	72%	-120%	$468,139.00	-37%	$340,530.00	-42%	$314,366.00	-37%
TOTALS:	624	473	151	76%	1135%	TOTAL:	214%	TOTAL:	171%	TOTAL:	154%

H) Parameters = Filter: B   Target price: 10%   Stop loss price: 30%   Time frame: 90 business days

YEAR	PICKS	WIN	LOSE	RATE	PROFIT	2 TRADES		3 TRADES		4 TRADES	
						PORTFOLIO	GAIN	PORTFOLIO	GAIN	PORTFOLIO	GAIN
2000	139	109	30	78%	235%	$107,256.00	7%	$109,034.00	9%	$113,956.00	14%
2001	65	50	15	77%	152%	$156,156.00	46%	$134,889.00	24%	$152,617.00	34%
2002	43	30	13	70%	80%	$172,615.00	11%	$158,984.00	18%	$167,686.00	10%
2003	22	18	4	82%	115%	$178,161.00	3%	$186,984.00	18%	$205,384.00	22%
2004	40	33	7	83%	203%	$192,015.00	8%	$219,016.00	17%	$252,781.00	23%
2005	38	28	10	74%	108%	$232,362.00	21%	$267,810.00	22%	$314,604.00	24%
2006	39	34	5	87%	238%	$346,643.00	49%	$406,406.00	52%	$463,126.00	47%
2007	65	43	22	66%	-60%	$296,401.00	-14%	$395,833.00	-3%	$427,780.00	-8%
2008	83	61	22	73%	-50%	$244,097.00	-18%	$269,023.00	-32%	$329,243.00	-23%
TOTALS:	534	406	128	76%	1021%	TOTAL:	113%	TOTAL:	125%	TOTAL:	143%

120

4. One Business Day

These statistics show the percentage of <u>winning</u> Tailwind trades that hit their target price in 1 business day. These statistics are cumulative from 2000 through 2008. Some years may be above or below these percentages.

Using Filter A, a 10% profit, 20% stop loss, and a 60 day time frame, there were 424 <u>winning</u> trades from 2000 through 2008, as shown in the table in Section 1. Of these 424 <u>winning</u> trades, 27 hit the 10% target price in 1 business day. That is 6%. You will find the details about all of these stocks in the detailed track record located at the end of this chapter.

Using Filter B, a 10% profit, 20% stop loss, and a 60 day time frame, there were 363 <u>winning</u> trades from 2000 through 2008, as shown in the table in Section 1. Of these 363 <u>winning</u> trades, 27 hit the 10% target price in 1 business day. That is 7%.

5. Five Business Days

These statistics show the percentage of <u>winning</u> Tailwind trades that hit their target price in 5 business days or less. These statistics are cumulative from 2000 through 2008. Some years may be above or below these percentages.

Using Filter A, a 10% profit, 20% stop loss, and a 60 day time frame, there were 424 <u>winning</u> trades from 2000 through 2008, as shown in the table in Section 1. Out of these 424 <u>winning</u> trades, 116 winning trades hit the 10% target price in 5 business days or less. That is 27%. You will find the details about all of these stocks in the detailed track record located at the end of this chapter.

Using Filter B, a 10% profit, 20% stop loss, and a 60 day time frame, there were 363 <u>winning</u> trades from 2000 through 2008, as shown in the table in Section 1. Of these 363 <u>winning</u> trades, 110 winning trades hit the 10% target price in 5 business days or less. That is 30%.

6. Fifteen Business Days

These statistics show the percentage of <u>winning</u> Tailwind trades that hit their target price in 15 business days or less. These statistics are cumulative from 2000 through 2008. Some years may be above or below these percentages.

Using Filter A, a 10% profit, 20% stop loss, and a 60 day time frame, there were 424 <u>winning</u> trades from 2000 through 2008, as shown in the table in Section 1. Of these 424 <u>winning</u> trades, 226 winning trades hit the 10% target price in 15 business days or less. That is 53%. You will find the details about all of these stocks in the detailed track record located at the end of this chapter.

Using Filter B, a 10% profit, 20% stop loss, and a 60 day time frame, there were 363 <u>winning</u> trades from 2000 through 2008, as shown in the table in Section 1. Of these 363 <u>winning</u> trades, 204 winning trades hit the 10% target price in 15 business days or less. That is 56%.

7. Detailed Track Record

The rest of this chapter contains the detailed track record for the Tailwind Trading System. <u>This track record shows the detailed results when using Filter A, a 10% profit, 20% stop loss, and a 60 day time frame.</u>

When a stock was closed out and the profit or loss was zero, it was counted as a loser. The stocks have been separated by year based on the date the stock was added to an S&P index. That is when the Tailwind "stock pick" was made. For example, a stock may have been added to an

S&P index on December 10th, 2000. That stock is counted in the year 2000 in the overall track records and the detailed track record, even though the buy date, Day 56, would occur sometime in 2001.

The track record is from 2000 through 2008. The keys to reading the columns of the tables are as follows:

YEAR - the year that is used to catalog and track the stock for the overall track records.

TICKER SYMBOL - the stock's ticker symbol.

DATE ADDED- the date the stock was added to an S&P index.

CLOSING PRICE - the stock's closing price on the effective date.

BUY DATE - the date the stock was purchased for the Tailwind Trading System, this is Day 56.

OPENING PRICE - the stock's opening price on the buy date, Day 56.

TARGET PRICE – the stock's 10% target price. The 10% target price is set at 10% above the OPENING PRICE.

STOP PRICE - the stock's 20% stop loss price. The stop loss price is set at 20% below the OPENING PRICE.

HIGH PRICE - the high price of the stock on the day it reaches the target price. If the stock price hits the stop loss price before it reaches the target price, then the letters "SO" are posted in the HIGH PRICE column. "SO" means "Stopped Out". If the stock price does not reach the target price or the stop loss price within the desired time frame from the buy date, which is 60 business days for the track record shown here, then the letters "CO" are posted in the HIGH PRICE column. "CO" means "Closed Out".

DATE - the date the high price was reached, or the date the stock was stopped out (SO), or the date the stock was closed out (CO).

W/L - shows whether the trade was a winning trade (W) or a losing trade (L).

DAYS - the number of <u>business days</u> it took for the stock to reach the target price, or the stop loss price, or to be closed out. The number of days is counted from the buy date, and includes the buy date. 60 business days was the time frame used for the track record shown here.

P/L - shows the profit or loss from the trade. A profit is shown in black; a loss is shown in red with a negative sign. Stocks that hit their target price show a 10% profit. Stocks that are stopped out show a 20% loss. Stocks that are closed out will show a profit or a loss based on the difference from the opening price of the stock on the buy date to the closing price of the stock on the sell date.

YEAR	TICKER SYMBOL	DATE ADDED	CLOSING PRICE	BUY DATE	OPENING PRICE	TARGET PRICE	STOP PRICE	HIGH PRICE	DATE	W/L	DAYS	P/L
2000	YNR	1/5/2000	$63.00	3/27/2000	$53.31	$58.64	$42.65	S.O	4/4/2000	L	7	-20%
2000	FYII	1/5/2000	$32.09	3/27/2000	$24.88	$27.37	$19.90	$28.31	3/31/2000	W	5	10%
2000	JAKK	1/7/2000	$24.63	3/29/2000	$19.13	$21.04	$15.30	$21.75	3/31/2000	W	3	10%
2000	BERW	1/11/2000	$42.38	3/31/2000	$35.88	$39.47	$28.70	$39.81	4/7/2000	W	6	10%
2000	SIB	1/13/2000	$9.00	4/4/2000	$8.69	$9.56	$6.95	C.O	6/28/2000	W	60	3%
2000	STLD	1/13/2000	$4.45	4/4/2000	$2.83	$3.11	$2.26	$3.11	4/10/2000	W	5	10%
2000	BIIB	1/28/2000	$42.75	4/18/2000	$22.25	$24.48	$17.80	$28.17	4/19/2000	W	2	10%
2000	CNXT	1/28/2000	$212.39	4/18/2000	$131.83	$145.01	$105.46	$146.24	4/19/2000	W	2	10%
2000	SY	1/28/2000	$23.81	4/18/2000	$18.81	$20.69	$15.05	$21.88	4/18/2000	W	1	10%
2000	TQNT	1/28/2000	$40.13	4/18/2000	$34.94	$38.43	$27.95	$39.85	4/18/2000	W	1	10%
2000	VOXX	1/28/2000	$50.00	4/18/2000	$34.13	$37.54	$27.30	$39.25	4/19/2000	W	2	10%
2000	SFP	2/8/2000	$59.28	4/28/2000	$42.94	$47.23	$34.35	$49.81	5/2/2000	W	3	10%
2000	RLI	2/9/2000	$16.00	5/1/2000	$16.07	$17.68	$12.86	$18.00	5/30/2000	W	21	10%
2000	APN	2/10/2000	$19.00	5/2/2000	$16.38	$18.02	$13.10	S.O	6/19/2000	L	34	-20%
2000	COHU	2/15/2000	$50.00	5/5/2000	$37.63	$41.39	$30.10	S.O	6/13/2000	L	27	-20%
2000	AGS	2/23/2000	$31.75	5/12/2000	$16.75	$18.43	$13.40	S.O	5/22/2000	L	7	-20%
2000	DEL	2/23/2000	$23.00	5/12/2000	$22.31	$24.54	$17.85	C.O	8/7/2000	L	60	-8%
2000	CHRW	2/29/2000	$12.75	5/18/2000	$11.53	$12.68	$9.22	$13.02	7/11/2000	W	37	10%
2000	CUNO	3/8/2000	$28.13	5/26/2000	$27.44	$30.18	$21.95	$30.25	7/31/2000	W	45	10%
2000	LG	3/8/2000	$19.72	5/26/2000	$19.19	$21.11	$15.35	C.O	8/21/2000	W	60	7%
2000	VCI	3/8/2000	$32.91	5/26/2000	$32.94	$36.23	$26.35	$37.13	6/15/2000	W	14	10%
2000	NVDA	3/13/2000	$12.44	6/1/2000	$9.79	$10.77	$7.83	$11.09	6/2/2000	W	2	10%
2000	CSGS	3/15/2000	$66.94	6/5/2000	$57.25	$62.98	$45.80	S.O	6/14/2000	L	8	-20%
2000	TXCC	3/22/2000	$117.75	6/12/2000	$84.50	$92.95	$67.60	S.O	7/5/2000	L	17	-20%
2000	MOR	3/23/2000	$15.94	6/13/2000	$15.88	$17.47	$12.70	$18.00	7/12/2000	W	21	10%
2000	RSYS	3/27/2000	$62.25	6/15/2000	$45.50	$50.05	$36.40	$50.25	6/15/2000	W	1	10%
2000	CRCL	3/29/2000	$26.63	6/19/2000	$19.19	$21.11	$15.35	$21.31	6/21/2000	W	3	10%
2000	VTS	3/29/2000	$29.75	6/19/2000	$25.38	$27.92	$20.30	S.O	7/31/2000	L	30	-20%
2000	LD	3/31/2000	$34.00	6/21/2000	$34.44	$37.88	$27.55	S.O	7/21/2000	L	22	-20%
2000	SRT	3/31/2000	$73.56	6/21/2000	$55.25	$60.78	$44.20	S.O	7/17/2000	L	18	-20%

Tailwind Trading System

Chapter 10: Track Records and Statistics

YEAR	TICKER SYMBOL	DATE ADDED	CLOSING PRICE	BUY DATE	OPENING PRICE	TARGET PRICE	STOP PRICE	HIGH PRICE	DATE	W/L	DAYS	P/L
2000	VRTS	3/31/2000	$131.00	6/21/2000	$134.88	$148.37	$107.90	S.O	6/29/2000	L	7	-20%
2000	TTN	4/7/2000	$53.50	6/28/2000	$44.81	$49.29	$35.85	S.O	7/11/2000	L	9	-20%
2000	ANTC	4/14/2000	$39.63	7/6/2000	$40.00	$44.00	$32.00	$44.00	7/10/2000	W	3	10%
2000	ARJ	4/17/2000	$21.94	7/7/2000	$20.81	$22.89	$16.65	C.O	9/29/2000	L	60	-12%
2000	EPRE	4/18/2000	$14.19	7/10/2000	$7.03	$7.73	$5.62	$8.50	7/11/2000	W	2	10%
2000	PEGS	4/19/2000	$15.81	7/11/2000	$11.13	$12.24	$8.90	$13.19	7/12/2000	W	2	10%
2000	PTEC	4/19/2000	$18.69	7/11/2000	$17.69	$19.46	$14.15	$20.06	7/13/2000	W	3	10%
2000	SCTC	4/19/2000	$23.06	7/11/2000	$18.00	$19.80	$14.40	$20.50	7/18/2000	W	6	10%
2000	UNS	4/26/2000	$15.38	7/17/2000	$15.12	$16.63	$12.10	$16.69	9/14/2000	W	43	10%
2000	NVR	5/2/2000	$62.00	7/21/2000	$61.88	$68.07	$49.50	$72.88	8/7/2000	W	12	10%
2000	MXIM	5/9/2000	$63.64	7/28/2000	$64.56	$71.02	$51.65	$75.17	8/11/2000	W	11	10%
2000	UGI	5/9/2000	$7.29	7/28/2000	$7.33	$8.06	$5.86	$8.10	9/29/2000	W	45	10%
2000	AVTC	5/10/2000	$11.44	7/31/2000	$5.50	$6.05	$4.40	$6.25	8/10/2000	W	9	10%
2000	DAVX	5/10/2000	$25.94	7/31/2000	$8.41	$9.25	$6.73	$9.50	8/1/2000	W	2	10%
2000	ASGN	5/12/2000	$28.94	8/2/2000	$27.38	$30.12	$21.90	$30.25	9/1/2000	W	23	10%
2000	ALSC	5/30/2000	$25.38	8/17/2000	$23.88	$26.27	$19.10	$26.44	8/25/2000	W	7	10%
2000	APCC	5/31/2000	$35.44	8/18/2000	$22.75	$25.03	$18.20	$25.25	8/28/2000	W	7	10%
2000	WFSL	5/31/2000	$12.69	8/18/2000	$12.57	$13.83	$10.06	$13.89	9/26/2000	W	27	10%
2000	PWR	6/7/2000	$56.88	8/25/2000	$43.44	$47.78	$34.75	$47.88	9/1/2000	W	6	10%
2000	NEV	6/9/2000	$20.50	8/29/2000	$18.75	$20.63	$15.00	$21.00	10/12/2000	W	32	10%
2000	CVG	6/12/2000	$46.69	8/30/2000	$41.06	$45.17	$32.85	$46.19	9/15/2000	W	12	10%
2000	GLC	6/12/2000	$26.75	8/30/2000	$18.00	$19.80	$14.40	S.O	10/5/2000	L	26	-20%
2000	ARXX	6/16/2000	$17.87	9/6/2000	$17.84	$19.62	$14.27	$19.75	9/7/2000	W	2	10%
2000	CF	6/16/2000	$24.50	9/6/2000	$23.19	$25.51	$18.55	C.O	11/29/2000	W	60	1%
2000	VAL	6/16/2000	$19.00	9/6/2000	$14.63	$16.09	$11.70	S.O	9/22/2000	L	13	-20%
2000	BKNG	6/20/2000	$17.38	9/8/2000	$17.31	$19.04	$13.85	$19.13	11/29/2000	W	58	10%
2000	HSII	6/23/2000	$57.00	9/13/2000	$43.59	$47.95	$34.87	$48.75	9/13/2000	W	1	10%
2000	VNWK	6/23/2000	$27.88	9/13/2000	$7.38	$8.12	$5.90	S.O	9/27/2000	L	11	-20%
2000	MHI	6/27/2000	$27.44	9/15/2000	$27.69	$30.46	$22.15	$31.13	10/27/2000	W	31	10%
2000	AWRE	6/28/2000	$52.50	9/18/2000	$42.06	$46.27	$33.65	S.O	10/6/2000	L	15	-20%

127

Tailwind Trading System

YEAR	TICKER SYMBOL	DATE ADDED	CLOSING PRICE	BUY DATE	OPENING PRICE	TARGET PRICE	STOP PRICE	HIGH PRICE	DATE	W/L	DAYS	P/L
2000	AVNT	6/30/2000	$18.73	9/20/2000	$17.31	$19.04	$13.85	C.O	12/13/2000	W	60	6%
2000	PLMD	6/30/2000	$21.63	9/20/2000	$20.44	$22.48	$16.35	$23.78	9/25/2000	W	4	10%
2000	SWS	6/30/2000	$18.55	9/20/2000	$18.15	$19.97	$14.52	S.O	10/3/2000	L	10	-20%
2000	VSAT	6/30/2000	$27.13	9/20/2000	$27.25	$29.98	$21.80	S.O	10/3/2000	L	10	-20%
2000	CIT	7/14/2000	$20.00	10/3/2000	$17.19	$18.91	$13.75	S.O	10/11/2000	L	7	-20%
2000	CGO	7/14/2000	$39.25	10/3/2000	$40.88	$44.97	$32.70	S.O	12/4/2000	L	44	-20%
2000	BRKT	7/20/2000	$29.94	10/9/2000	$22.11	$24.32	$17.69	$26.89	10/9/2000	W	1	10%
2000	AVA	7/25/2000	$19.75	10/12/2000	$19.00	$20.90	$15.20	$21.13	10/13/2000	W	2	10%
2000	SCHS	7/26/2000	$17.31	10/13/2000	$18.00	$19.80	$14.40	$20.00	10/17/2000	W	3	10%
2000	FTUS	7/27/2000	$40.75	10/16/2000	$29.44	$32.38	$23.55	$32.38	10/20/2000	W	5	10%
2000	FWRD	7/27/2000	$28.79	10/16/2000	$25.00	$27.50	$20.00	$27.79	10/26/2000	W	9	10%
2000	ROBV	7/27/2000	$15.19	10/16/2000	$4.75	$5.23	$3.80	$5.31	10/16/2000	W	1	10%
2000	CMOS	8/2/2000	$48.77	10/20/2000	$18.13	$19.94	$14.50	$20.38	10/23/2000	W	2	10%
2000	GBCB	8/2/2000	$35.00	10/20/2000	$29.81	$32.79	$23.85	$33.25	11/1/2000	W	9	10%
2000	NUI	8/8/2000	$29.44	10/26/2000	$28.88	$31.77	$23.10	$32.63	12/27/2000	W	43	10%
2000	TA	8/9/2000	$20.94	10/27/2000	$20.75	$22.83	$16.60	$23.13	10/31/2000	W	3	10%
2000	CHS	8/10/2000	$3.72	10/30/2000	$3.51	$3.86	$2.81	$3.88	10/30/2000	W	1	10%
2000	DSPG	8/24/2000	$43.58	11/13/2000	$21.60	$23.76	$17.28	$25.69	11/14/2000	W	2	10%
2000	LSCC	8/29/2000	$35.69	11/16/2000	$21.38	$23.52	$17.10	S.O	11/28/2000	L	8	-20%
2000	IRF	8/31/2000	$62.84	11/20/2000	$37.88	$41.67	$30.30	S.O	11/30/2000	L	8	-20%
2000	KDE	8/31/2000	$21.00	11/20/2000	$13.06	$14.37	$10.45	S.O	12/1/2000	L	9	-20%
2000	MEAD	8/31/2000	$24.00	11/20/2000	$9.81	$10.79	$7.85	S.O	12/6/2000	L	12	-20%
2000	GBBK	9/7/2000	$30.75	11/27/2000	$32.00	$35.20	$25.60	$35.63	12/5/2000	W	7	10%
2000	SFY	9/7/2000	$35.50	11/27/2000	$35.06	$38.57	$28.05	$39.50	12/28/2000	W	23	10%
2000	BCF	9/12/2000	$15.50	11/30/2000	$14.13	$15.54	$11.30	$16.00	12/7/2000	W	6	10%
2000	INFS	9/14/2000	$53.44	12/4/2000	$31.50	$34.65	$25.20	$35.44	12/6/2000	W	3	10%
2000	CAI	9/20/2000	$11.57	12/8/2000	$11.50	$12.65	$9.20	$12.88	1/16/2001	W	25	10%
2000	NYFX	9/25/2000	$40.20	12/13/2000	$30.00	$33.00	$24.00	S.O	12/18/2000	L	4	-20%
2000	SPSS	9/26/2000	$28.69	12/14/2000	$19.22	$21.14	$15.38	$21.88	12/19/2000	W	4	10%
2000	URI	9/28/2000	$23.63	12/18/2000	$14.75	$16.23	$11.80	S.O	12/21/2000	L	4	-20%

128

YEAR	TICKER SYMBOL	DATE ADDED	CLOSING PRICE	BUY DATE	OPENING PRICE	TARGET PRICE	STOP PRICE	HIGH PRICE	DATE	W/L	DAYS	P/L
2000	PRHC	9/29/2000	$39.94	12/19/2000	$37.06	$40.77	$29.65	$41.88	12/26/2000	W	5	10%
2000	SIVB	9/29/2000	$58.22	12/19/2000	$33.22	$36.54	$26.58	$37.00	12/19/2000	W	1	10%
2000	AAS	10/2/2000	$49.19	12/20/2000	$47.94	$52.73	$38.35	$53.44	12/28/2000	W	6	10%
2000	DYN	10/2/2000	$52.92	12/20/2000	$51.07	$56.18	$40.86	$56.54	12/26/2000	W	4	10%
2000	EAGL	10/2/2000	$31.00	12/20/2000	$20.81	$22.89	$16.65	$23.81	12/27/2000	W	5	10%
2000	LRCX	10/2/2000	$22.75	12/20/2000	$14.13	$15.54	$11.30	$15.56	12/26/2000	W	4	10%
2000	PSEM	10/2/2000	$42.75	12/20/2000	$15.69	$17.26	$12.55	$18.38	12/22/2000	W	3	10%
2000	HAKI	10/4/2000	$27.00	12/22/2000	$18.00	$19.80	$14.40	$20.72	12/28/2000	W	4	10%
2000	PACW	10/4/2000	$11.95	12/22/2000	$3.25	$3.58	$2.60	$3.75	12/22/2000	W	1	10%
2000	KFY	10/6/2000	$39.88	12/27/2000	$20.25	$22.28	$16.20	$23.38	1/3/2001	W	5	10%
2000	PR	10/26/2000	$21.00	1/18/2001	$18.00	$19.80	$14.40	$19.98	1/31/2001	W	10	10%
2000	PDLI	10/31/2000	$67.53	1/23/2001	$29.25	$32.18	$23.40	$33.69	1/23/2001	W	1	10%
2000	VRTX	10/31/2000	$93.09	1/23/2001	$60.31	$66.34	$48.25	$69.31	1/23/2001	W	1	10%
2000	DY	11/1/2000	$39.69	1/24/2001	$30.06	$33.07	$24.05	$33.44	1/24/2001	W	1	10%
2000	HLIT	11/1/2000	$15.38	1/24/2001	$9.75	$10.73	$7.80	$11.19	1/24/2001	W	1	10%
2000	PCTI	11/2/2000	$19.00	1/25/2001	$12.03	$13.23	$9.62	S.O	2/23/2001	L	21	-20%
2000	POS	11/3/2000	$39.63	1/26/2001	$32.00	$35.20	$25.60	$35.73	1/30/2001	W	3	10%
2000	IHI	11/3/2000	$34.25	1/26/2001	$25.25	$27.78	$20.20	S.O	3/27/2001	L	42	-20%
2000	RDN	11/7/2000	$33.00	1/30/2001	$32.50	$35.75	$26.00	C.O	4/25/2001	W	60	6%
2000	RNBO	11/7/2000	$25.69	1/30/2001	$12.88	$14.17	$10.30	S.O	2/12/2001	L	10	-20%
2000	CRY	11/9/2000	$28.51	2/1/2001	$26.52	$29.17	$21.22	$29.25	2/13/2001	W	9	10%
2000	KOPN	11/20/2000	$14.88	2/12/2001	$13.00	$14.30	$10.40	$14.56	2/13/2001	W	2	10%
2000	AFCI	11/28/2000	$31.38	2/20/2001	$21.63	$23.79	$17.30	S.O	3/5/2001	L	10	-20%
2000	BELM	11/28/2000	$21.17	2/20/2001	$17.09	$18.80	$13.67	S.O	3/1/2001	L	8	-20%
2000	RADS	11/28/2000	$21.50	2/20/2001	$19.03	$20.93	$15.22	S.O	3/12/2001	L	15	-20%
2000	IFCI	11/30/2000	$11.69	2/22/2001	$5.63	$6.19	$4.50	S.O	3/16/2001	L	17	-20%
2000	KEM	11/30/2000	$17.50	2/22/2001	$17.50	$19.25	$14.00	$19.90	3/6/2001	W	9	10%
2000	SCMM	11/30/2000	$34.31	2/22/2001	$23.38	$25.72	$18.70	S.O	2/27/2001	L	4	-20%
2000	BCGI	12/4/2000	$24.63	2/26/2001	$7.94	$8.73	$6.35	S.O	3/1/2001	L	4	-20%
2000	BELFB	12/4/2000	$37.69	2/26/2001	$31.81	$34.99	$25.45	S.O	3/12/2001	L	11	-20%

129

Chapter 10: Track Records and Statistics

YEAR	TICKER SYMBOL	DATE ADDED	CLOSING PRICE	BUY DATE	OPENING PRICE	TARGET PRICE	STOP PRICE	HIGH PRICE	DATE	W/L	DAYS	P/L
2000	CORR	12/4/2000	$41.44	2/26/2001	$33.50	$36.85	$26.80	$37.13	2/27/2001	W	2	10%
2000	RFMD	12/4/2000	$26.94	2/26/2001	$13.44	$14.78	$10.75	S.O	3/1/2001	L	4	-20%
2000	RHI	12/4/2000	$32.06	2/26/2001	$24.00	$26.40	$19.20	$28.00	4/18/2001	W	37	10%
2000	ABK	12/8/2000	$56.28	3/2/2001	$55.75	$61.33	$44.60	$61.85	3/8/2001	W	5	10%
2000	ACDO	12/8/2000	$24.50	3/2/2001	$18.00	$19.80	$14.40	$20.00	3/19/2001	W	12	10%
2000	INTU	12/8/2000	$24.57	3/2/2001	$21.32	$23.45	$17.06	$23.53	3/7/2001	W	4	10%
2000	MIPS	12/8/2000	$36.59	3/2/2001	$30.44	$33.48	$24.35	$33.94	3/6/2001	W	3	10%
2000	MVSN	12/8/2000	$70.69	3/2/2001	$36.94	$40.63	$29.55	$46.31	3/2/2001	W	1	10%
2000	PLT	12/8/2000	$46.88	3/2/2001	$25.64	$28.20	$20.51	S.O	3/20/2001	L	13	-20%
2000	ROG	12/8/2000	$43.50	3/2/2001	$34.80	$38.28	$27.84	S.O	4/6/2001	L	26	-20%
2000	SUPX	12/8/2000	$26.13	3/2/2001	$13.75	$15.13	$11.00	$15.38	3/2/2001	W	1	10%
2000	BRL	12/11/2000	$31.44	3/5/2001	$25.49	$28.04	$20.39	S.O	3/22/2001	L	14	-20%
2000	PLXS	12/11/2000	$54.50	3/5/2001	$34.84	$38.32	$27.87	$39.75	3/6/2001	W	2	10%
2000	QLGC	12/11/2000	$59.97	3/5/2001	$18.00	$19.80	$14.40	$22.44	3/6/2001	W	2	10%
2000	ULTE	12/11/2000	$27.94	3/5/2001	$25.38	$27.92	$20.30	$28.50	3/20/2001	W	12	10%
2000	VTSS	12/11/2000	$64.25	3/5/2001	$37.19	$40.91	$29.75	$45.25	3/6/2001	W	2	10%
2000	AEIS	12/12/2000	$25.56	3/6/2001	$25.50	$28.05	$20.40	$30.00	3/23/2001	W	14	10%
2000	AJG	12/12/2000	$33.50	3/6/2001	$27.41	$30.15	$21.93	C.O	5/30/2001	W	60	1%
2000	CPS	12/12/2000	$30.88	3/6/2001	$26.88	$29.57	$21.50	$30.00	5/17/2001	W	52	10%
2000	EXPD	12/12/2000	$14.22	3/6/2001	$14.03	$15.43	$11.22	S.O	3/16/2001	L	9	-20%
2000	GCO	12/12/2000	$23.94	3/6/2001	$24.25	$26.68	$19.40	$27.00	3/7/2001	W	2	10%
2000	IFIN	12/12/2000	$44.09	3/6/2001	$39.56	$43.52	$31.65	S.O	3/19/2001	L	10	-20%
2000	JKHY	12/12/2000	$29.44	3/6/2001	$23.69	$26.06	$18.95	$26.25	3/14/2001	W	7	10%
2000	CYMI	12/13/2000	$26.63	3/7/2001	$23.78	$26.16	$19.02	S.O	3/19/2001	L	9	-20%
2000	PFCB	12/15/2000	$18.28	3/9/2001	$17.13	$18.84	$13.70	$18.94	4/3/2001	W	18	10%
2000	WMS	12/15/2000	$13.13	3/9/2001	$12.51	$13.76	$10.01	$14.13	4/30/2001	W	36	10%
2000	RARE	12/18/2000	$18.00	3/12/2001	$18.41	$20.25	$14.73	S.O	3/23/2001	L	10	-20%
2000	ARTC	12/20/2000	$18.00	3/14/2001	$13.50	$14.85	$10.80	$14.94	3/14/2001	W	1	10%
2000	IMPH	12/20/2000	$56.94	3/14/2001	$43.88	$48.27	$35.10	$49.50	3/14/2001	W	1	10%
2000	MOGN	12/20/2000	$9.97	3/14/2001	$5.03	$5.53	$4.02	S.O	3/16/2001	L	3	-20%

YEAR	TICKER SYMBOL	DATE ADDED	CLOSING PRICE	BUY DATE	OPENING PRICE	TARGET PRICE	STOP PRICE	HIGH PRICE	DATE	W/L	DAYS	P/L
2000	NATI	12/20/2000	$32.29	3/14/2001	$26.83	$29.51	$21.46	S.O	3/20/2001	L	5	-20%
2000	APWR	12/28/2000	$33.94	3/21/2001	$30.63	$33.69	$24.50	$35.44	3/26/2001	W	4	10%
2000	SBIB	12/28/2000	$8.87	3/21/2001	$7.60	$8.36	$6.08	C.O	6/14/2001	L	60	-3%
2000	AMCC	12/29/2000	$300.12	3/22/2001	$80.76	$88.84	$64.61	$97.00	3/22/2001	W	1	10%
2001	MRL	1/8/2001	$26.69	3/29/2001	$27.72	$30.49	$22.18	$30.73	4/30/2001	W	22	10%
2001	FED	1/10/2001	$29.75	4/2/2001	$27.90	$30.69	$22.32	$31.15	4/18/2001	W	12	10%
2001	BFT	2/1/2001	$30.15	4/24/2001	$25.80	$28.38	$20.64	$29.25	6/21/2001	W	42	10%
2001	LAB	2/6/2001	$47.29	4/27/2001	$35.10	$38.61	$28.08	$38.80	5/1/2001	W	3	10%
2001	FRNT	2/21/2001	$25.50	5/11/2001	$14.99	$16.49	$11.99	$16.54	5/21/2001	W	7	10%
2001	CZN	2/26/2001	$15.70	5/16/2001	$13.36	$14.70	$10.69	$14.75	5/21/2001	W	4	10%
2001	KP	2/27/2001	$21.55	5/17/2001	$20.00	$22.00	$16.00	S.O	6/27/2001	L	29	-20%
2001	NEWP	2/28/2001	$48.88	5/18/2001	$37.88	$41.67	$30.30	$42.00	5/22/2001	W	3	10%
2001	AH	3/5/2001	$16.96	5/23/2001	$12.20	$13.42	$9.76	$13.80	6/4/2001	W	8	10%
2001	CHUX	3/22/2001	$19.69	6/12/2001	$18.18	$20.00	$14.54	$20.35	6/29/2001	W	14	10%
2001	POWI	3/22/2001	$17.42	6/12/2001	$14.19	$15.61	$11.35	$16.30	6/28/2001	W	13	10%
2001	NDE	3/26/2001	$28.61	6/14/2001	$25.73	$28.30	$20.58	$28.92	8/14/2001	W	43	10%
2001	MDU	3/27/2001	$15.24	6/15/2001	$14.94	$16.43	$11.95	C.O	9/10/2001	L	60	-19%
2001	HAE	3/28/2001	$30.85	6/18/2001	$31.10	$34.21	$24.88	$34.50	8/7/2001	W	36	10%
2001	ELNT	3/30/2001	$26.56	6/20/2001	$23.40	$25.74	$18.72	$27.12	6/27/2001	W	6	10%
2001	EQT	3/30/2001	$17.25	6/20/2001	$16.67	$18.34	$13.34	C.O	9/19/2001	L	60	-16%
2001	HCC	4/11/2001	$18.73	7/2/2001	$16.49	$18.14	$13.19	C.O	10/1/2001	W	60	4%
2001	WGR	4/16/2001	$18.71	7/5/2001	$16.23	$17.85	$12.98	S.O	9/24/2001	L	53	-20%
2001	HOTT	4/30/2001	$14.85	7/19/2001	$13.22	$14.54	$10.58	$14.84	8/16/2001	W	21	10%
2001	PBG	5/11/2001	$22.15	8/1/2001	$21.73	$23.90	$17.38	$24.32	10/2/2001	W	40	10%
2001	KSU	5/23/2001	$16.75	8/13/2001	$13.75	$15.13	$11.00	S.O	9/20/2001	L	24	-20%
2001	SBSE	5/23/2001	$22.06	8/13/2001	$17.55	$19.31	$14.04	S.O	8/15/2001	L	3	-20%
2001	CBK	5/25/2001	$19.50	8/15/2001	$11.77	$12.95	$9.42	$14.37	9/6/2001	W	16	10%
2001	ADVS	5/31/2001	$65.26	8/20/2001	$54.00	$59.40	$43.20	S.O	9/17/2001	L	16	-20%
2001	LTXX	6/5/2001	$28.25	8/23/2001	$17.70	$19.47	$14.16	S.O	9/17/2001	L	13	-20%
2001	WGOV	6/8/2001	$14.94	8/28/2001	$12.50	$13.75	$10.00	S.O	9/18/2001	L	11	-20%

131

YEAR	TICKER SYMBOL	DATE ADDED	CLOSING PRICE	BUY DATE	OPENING PRICE	TARGET PRICE	STOP PRICE	HIGH PRICE	DATE	W/L	DAYS	P/L
2001	CATT	6/14/2001	$27.40	9/4/2001	$18.05	$19.86	$14.44	S.O	9/10/2001	L	5	-20%
2001	CNB	6/22/2001	$14.75	9/18/2001	$12.10	$13.31	$9.68	$13.58	11/6/2001	W	36	10%
2001	ZION	6/22/2001	$57.55	9/18/2001	$53.78	$59.16	$43.02	S.O	10/15/2001	L	20	-20%
2001	JHF	6/27/2001	$40.00	9/21/2001	$35.60	$39.16	$28.48	$40.00	9/28/2001	W	6	10%
2001	CENX	7/6/2001	$18.77	10/1/2001	$8.59	$9.45	$6.87	$9.72	10/2/2001	W	2	10%
2001	RSAS	7/6/2001	$26.59	10/1/2001	$10.88	$11.97	$8.70	$12.75	10/1/2001	W	1	10%
2001	FRC	7/11/2001	$16.10	10/4/2001	$14.41	$15.85	$11.53	$16.13	12/6/2001	W	45	10%
2001	BEIQ	7/18/2001	$28.44	10/11/2001	$19.87	$21.86	$15.90	S.O	11/8/2001	L	21	-20%
2001	FEIC	7/19/2001	$39.88	10/12/2001	$29.36	$32.30	$23.49	S.O	10/19/2001	L	6	-20%
2001	TTWO	7/31/2001	$13.24	10/24/2001	$7.98	$8.78	$6.38	$9.45	10/26/2001	W	3	10%
2001	PMCS	8/2/2001	$36.87	10/26/2001	$18.05	$19.86	$14.44	$20.79	11/8/2001	W	10	10%
2001	UNT	8/2/2001	$13.06	10/26/2001	$11.25	$12.38	$9.00	$12.40	11/13/2001	W	13	10%
2001	FDO	8/3/2001	$28.24	10/29/2001	$29.43	$32.37	$23.54	$32.90	1/23/2002	W	59	10%
2001	TWAV	8/7/2001	$15.48	10/31/2001	$12.30	$13.53	$9.84	$13.84	12/5/2001	W	25	10%
2001	TGI	8/22/2001	$47.97	11/15/2001	$27.60	$30.36	$22.08	$30.48	11/26/2001	W	7	10%
2001	DCOM	8/28/2001	$11.63	11/21/2001	$10.97	$12.07	$8.78	$12.11	12/6/2001	W	11	10%
2001	FNF	8/28/2001	$5.29	11/21/2001	$5.02	$5.52	$4.02	$5.54	1/15/2002	W	37	10%
2001	ESA	8/29/2001	$17.30	11/23/2001	$14.74	$16.21	$11.79	$16.48	12/5/2001	W	9	10%
2001	FST	8/31/2001	$17.72	11/27/2001	$16.94	$18.63	$13.55	$18.73	12/24/2001	W	20	10%
2001	EXAR	9/5/2001	$20.66	11/29/2001	$20.45	$22.50	$16.36	$24.45	12/5/2001	W	5	10%
2001	HSIC	9/20/2001	$18.84	12/10/2001	$19.52	$21.47	$15.62	$21.81	1/22/2002	W	29	10%
2001	CYTC	9/28/2001	$26.81	12/18/2001	$26.26	$28.89	$21.01	S.O	1/30/2002	L	29	-20%
2001	SFG	9/28/2001	$24.20	12/18/2001	$23.70	$26.07	$18.96	$26.20	2/7/2002	W	35	10%
2001	MKT	10/5/2001	$19.02	12/26/2001	$17.30	$19.03	$13.84	$19.10	12/27/2001	W	2	10%
2001	MXT	10/5/2001	$27.91	12/26/2001	$24.64	$27.10	$19.71	$27.99	12/28/2001	W	3	10%
2001	STC	10/5/2001	$21.26	12/26/2001	$19.98	$21.98	$15.98	C.O	3/22/2002	L	60	-2%
2001	CLP	10/9/2001	$25.35	12/28/2001	$25.85	$28.44	$20.68	$28.46	2/28/2002	W	42	10%
2001	EDMC	10/9/2001	$18.19	12/28/2001	$18.90	$20.79	$15.12	$20.83	3/4/2002	W	44	10%
2001	EOP	10/9/2001	$30.75	12/28/2001	$29.97	$32.97	$23.98	C.O	3/26/2002	L	60	0%
2001	ICBC	10/9/2001	$22.95	12/28/2001	$23.27	$25.60	$18.62	$26.05	1/24/2002	W	18	10%

Tailwind Trading System

Chapter 10: Track Records and Statistics

YEAR	TICKER SYMBOL	DATE ADDED	CLOSING PRICE	BUY DATE	OPENING PRICE	TARGET PRICE	STOP PRICE	HIGH PRICE	DATE	W/L	DAYS	P/L
2001	KRC	10/9/2001	$24.25	12/28/2001	$25.30	$27.83	$20.24	$28.00	3/15/2002	W	53	10%
2001	NXL	10/9/2001	$18.94	12/28/2001	$19.20	$21.12	$15.36	C.O	3/26/2002	W	60	6%
2001	SHU	10/9/2001	$31.05	12/28/2001	$32.25	$35.48	$25.80	C.O	3/26/2002	W	60	6%
2001	TE	10/9/2001	$26.80	12/28/2001	$25.92	$28.51	$20.74	C.O	3/26/2002	W	60	8%
2001	NYCB	10/10/2001	$26.00	12/31/2001	$22.74	$25.01	$18.19	$25.06	1/9/2002	W	7	10%
2001	TWB	10/31/2001	$26.61	1/23/2002	$25.49	$28.04	$20.39	$28.45	2/21/2002	W	21	10%
2001	WCNX	10/31/2001	$29.22	1/23/2002	$26.51	$29.16	$21.21	$29.49	2/25/2002	W	23	10%
2001	BPFH	11/2/2001	$21.13	1/25/2002	$21.85	$24.04	$17.48	$24.50	3/4/2002	W	26	10%
2001	HMA	11/6/2001	$9.86	1/29/2002	$9.46	$10.41	$7.57	$10.43	3/28/2002	W	42	10%
2001	PLFE	11/20/2001	$20.09	2/12/2002	$20.30	$22.33	$16.24	$22.49	3/13/2002	W	21	10%
2001	TLGD	11/20/2001	$31.32	2/12/2002	$21.96	$24.16	$17.57	$25.00	3/7/2002	W	17	10%
2001	UHS	11/20/2001	$43.34	2/12/2002	$42.52	$46.77	$34.02	$46.99	4/19/2002	W	47	10%
2001	RTEC	11/28/2001	$37.30	2/20/2002	$38.16	$41.98	$30.53	$42.75	3/4/2002	W	9	10%
2001	ISSX	11/29/2001	$32.64	2/21/2002	$28.70	$31.57	$22.96	S.O	2/28/2002	L	6	-20%
2001	MCDTA	11/29/2001	$25.06	2/21/2002	$19.30	$21.23	$15.44	S.O	2/28/2002	L	6	-20%
2001	NVDA	11/29/2001	$17.87	2/21/2002	$18.53	$20.38	$14.82	S.O	3/28/2002	L	26	-20%
2001	EQR	11/30/2001	$28.95	2/22/2002	$26.35	$28.99	$21.08	$28.99	3/8/2002	W	11	10%
2001	MANH	12/6/2001	$33.62	2/28/2002	$30.63	$33.69	$24.50	$35.50	3/4/2002	W	3	10%
2001	SFD	12/6/2001	$25.75	2/28/2002	$25.16	$27.68	$20.13	S.O	5/7/2002	L	48	-20%
2001	GENZ	12/13/2001	$57.77	3/7/2002	$43.30	$47.63	$34.64	$48.10	3/13/2002	W	5	10%
2001	RSG	12/13/2001	$12.70	3/7/2002	$12.37	$13.61	$9.90	$13.64	5/13/2002	W	47	10%
2001	NETE	12/14/2001	$19.33	3/8/2002	$15.48	$17.03	$12.38	$17.30	3/8/2002	W	1	10%
2001	TBL	12/14/2001	$18.35	3/8/2002	$18.67	$20.54	$14.94	$20.80	3/27/2002	W	14	10%
2001	FCS	12/31/2001	$28.20	3/22/2002	$28.20	$31.02	$22.56	$32.03	4/17/2002	W	18	10%
2001	WAT	12/31/2001	$38.75	3/22/2002	$28.05	$30.86	$22.44	C.O	6/17/2002	L	60	-12%
2002	PCL	1/16/2002	$30.45	4/9/2002	$29.50	$32.45	$23.60	C.O	7/2/2002	W	60	1%
2002	CPRT	1/31/2002	$22.60	4/23/2002	$16.20	$17.82	$12.96	C.O	7/17/2002	L	60	-12%
2002	EFDS	1/31/2002	$17.44	4/23/2002	$17.71	$19.48	$14.17	S.O	5/21/2002	L	21	-20%
2002	RATL	1/31/2002	$23.48	4/23/2002	$15.48	$17.03	$12.38	S.O	5/3/2002	L	9	-20%
2002	ANSS	2/21/2002	$6.16	5/13/2002	$6.25	$6.88	$5.00	$7.32	5/20/2002	W	6	10%

133

YEAR	TICKER SYMBOL	DATE ADDED	CLOSING PRICE	BUY DATE	OPENING PRICE	TARGET PRICE	STOP PRICE	HIGH PRICE	DATE	W/L	DAYS	P/L
2002	EDO	3/1/2002	$28.25	5/21/2002	$28.25	$31.08	$22.60	S.O	7/3/2002	L	31	-20%
2002	UCI	3/26/2002	$18.20	6/14/2002	$17.26	$18.99	$13.81	$19.58	6/21/2002	W	6	10%
2002	CAKE	4/24/2002	$27.02	7/15/2002	$21.23	$23.35	$16.98	$23.86	7/25/2002	W	9	10%
2002	ESS	4/24/2002	$51.65	7/15/2002	$49.50	$54.45	$39.60	C.O	10/7/2002	L	60	-4%
2002	MIK	4/24/2002	$19.92	7/15/2002	$18.45	$20.30	$14.76	$20.30	8/14/2002	W	23	10%
2002	PLCE	4/24/2002	$36.48	7/15/2002	$24.90	$27.39	$19.92	S.O	7/31/2002	L	13	-20%
2002	SHFL	4/24/2002	$10.56	7/15/2002	$8.78	$9.66	$7.02	S.O	7/22/2002	L	6	-20%
2002	FTO	5/1/2002	$5.55	7/22/2002	$3.72	$4.09	$2.98	S.O	9/19/2002	L	43	-20%
2002	FTN	5/3/2002	$39.01	7/24/2002	$30.95	$34.05	$24.76	$34.50	7/24/2002	W	1	10%
2002	PATH	5/3/2002	$29.43	7/24/2002	$14.22	$15.64	$11.38	$16.29	7/31/2002	W	6	10%
2002	STZ	5/3/2002	$15.30	7/24/2002	$12.45	$13.70	$9.96	$14.17	7/25/2002	W	2	10%
2002	ADVP	5/10/2002	$31.31	7/31/2002	$21.51	$23.66	$17.21	S.O	8/1/2002	L	2	-20%
2002	ASD	5/10/2002	$25.31	7/31/2002	$24.05	$26.46	$19.24	C.O	10/23/2002	L	60	-5%
2002	FLIR	5/10/2002	$5.64	7/31/2002	$5.30	$5.83	$4.24	S.O	10/1/2002	L	44	-20%
2002	APOL	5/14/2002	$37.56	8/2/2002	$38.37	$42.21	$30.70	$43.27	8/16/2002	W	11	10%
2002	BJS	5/14/2002	$19.33	8/2/2002	$15.20	$16.72	$12.16	$17.40	8/15/2002	W	10	10%
2002	DIAN	5/14/2002	$65.97	8/2/2002	$38.60	$42.46	$30.88	$45.62	8/9/2002	W	6	10%
2002	DRD	5/14/2002	$35.28	8/2/2002	$14.80	$16.28	$11.84	$16.52	8/29/2002	W	20	10%
2002	ISIL	5/14/2002	$30.21	8/2/2002	$19.15	$21.07	$15.32	$21.25	8/22/2002	W	15	10%
2002	VAR	5/14/2002	$23.09	8/2/2002	$20.42	$22.46	$16.34	$22.90	10/3/2002	W	44	10%
2002	WFMI	5/14/2002	$25.06	8/2/2002	$21.25	$23.38	$17.00	$24.49	8/15/2002	W	10	10%
2002	HVT	6/12/2002	$19.15	8/30/2002	$12.50	$13.75	$10.00	$13.85	9/5/2002	W	4	10%
2002	JILL	6/12/2002	$23.83	8/30/2002	$23.70	$26.07	$18.96	S.O	9/30/2002	L	21	-20%
2002	TALX	6/12/2002	$8.25	8/30/2002	$5.91	$6.50	$4.73	$6.50	9/25/2002	W	18	10%
2002	AMH	6/14/2002	$38.40	9/4/2002	$31.35	$34.49	$25.08	C.O	11/26/2002	L	60	-1%
2002	MVK	7/11/2002	$14.45	9/30/2002	$9.02	$9.92	$7.22	$11.00	10/15/2002	W	12	10%
2002	GLB	7/24/2002	$19.20	10/11/2002	$18.89	$20.78	$15.11	C.O	1/7/2003	L	60	-5%
2002	VARI	8/1/2002	$32.62	10/21/2002	$30.85	$33.94	$24.68	C.O	1/15/2003	L	60	-8%
2002	CARS	8/5/2002	$24.35	10/23/2002	$24.18	$26.60	$19.34	C.O	1/17/2003	L	60	-5%
2002	RKT	8/15/2002	$16.10	11/4/2002	$12.40	$13.64	$9.92	$13.65	12/12/2002	W	28	10%

Chapter 10: Track Records and Statistics

YEAR	TICKER SYMBOL	DATE ADDED	CLOSING PRICE	BUY DATE	OPENING PRICE	TARGET PRICE	STOP PRICE	HIGH PRICE	DATE	W/L	DAYS	P/L
2002	CRL	9/3/2002	$38.95	11/20/2002	$38.10	$41.91	$30.48	S.O	1/14/2003	L	37	-20%
2002	RJR	9/3/2002	$58.00	11/20/2002	$39.60	$43.56	$31.68	$43.61	1/8/2003	W	33	10%
2002	AGP	9/30/2002	$16.77	12/18/2002	$14.18	$15.60	$11.34	$16.05	12/30/2002	W	8	10%
2002	IFC	9/30/2002	$17.00	12/18/2002	$16.85	$18.54	$13.48	$18.91	3/17/2003	W	60	10%
2002	WHES	9/30/2002	$17.30	12/18/2002	$14.99	$16.49	$11.99	$17.02	2/10/2003	W	36	10%
2002	CECO	10/1/2002	$25.52	12/19/2002	$19.47	$21.42	$15.58	$23.29	1/29/2003	W	27	10%
2002	HYDL	10/11/2002	$25.48	1/2/2003	$23.70	$26.07	$18.96	$26.68	2/26/2003	W	38	10%
2002	GISX	11/14/2002	$20.70	2/6/2003	$18.20	$20.02	$14.56	C.O	5/2/2003	W	60	8%
2002	CIMA	12/6/2002	$28.15	2/28/2003	$20.65	$22.72	$16.52	$23.06	4/4/2003	W	26	10%
2002	OVER	12/6/2002	$28.53	2/28/2003	$15.71	$17.28	$12.57	$17.45	3/5/2003	W	4	10%
2002	DGX	12/11/2002	$29.50	3/5/2003	$25.77	$28.35	$20.62	$28.80	3/21/2003	W	13	10%
2002	LRY	12/11/2002	$31.35	3/5/2003	$30.60	$33.66	$24.48	$33.68	5/23/2003	W	57	10%
2003	CSTR	1/13/2003	$24.96	4/3/2003	$15.75	$17.33	$12.60	$17.69	4/16/2003	W	10	10%
2003	TOL	1/13/2003	$10.72	4/3/2003	$10.49	$11.54	$8.39	$11.59	4/28/2003	W	17	10%
2003	CUB	1/17/2003	$22.60	4/9/2003	$16.87	$18.56	$13.50	$19.00	4/23/2003	W	10	10%
2003	AMB	1/27/2003	$26.85	4/16/2003	$27.68	$30.45	$22.14	C.O	7/11/2003	L	60	-2%
2003	INVN	1/27/2003	$26.60	4/16/2003	$22.50	$24.75	$18.00	$24.79	5/8/2003	W	16	10%
2003	AMMD	2/14/2003	$8.55	5/7/2003	$8.32	$9.15	$6.66	$9.15	7/7/2003	W	42	10%
2003	AIV	3/13/2003	$36.50	6/3/2003	$35.20	$38.72	$28.16	$39.20	7/30/2003	W	41	10%
2003	POSS	3/13/2003	$17.26	6/3/2003	$16.86	$18.55	$13.49	S.O	6/30/2003	L	20	-20%
2003	NLS	3/19/2003	$15.19	6/9/2003	$12.40	$13.64	$9.92	C.O	9/2/2003	L	60	-3%
2003	CYH	3/28/2003	$20.61	6/18/2003	$19.80	$21.78	$15.84	$22.55	7/29/2003	W	29	10%
2003	FIC	3/28/2003	$33.57	6/18/2003	$34.42	$37.86	$27.54	$38.31	7/25/2003	W	27	10%
2003	CCRN	7/28/2003	$14.50	10/15/2003	$14.40	$15.84	$11.52	$15.90	1/2/2004	W	55	10%
2003	BRKL	8/7/2003	$15.33	10/27/2003	$14.83	$16.31	$11.86	C.O	1/22/2004	W	60	4%
2003	EPIQ	8/19/2003	$12.44	11/6/2003	$11.66	$12.83	$9.33	$12.83	1/16/2004	W	49	10%
2003	IRN	8/27/2003	$17.35	11/14/2003	$11.00	$12.10	$8.80	$12.24	1/13/2004	W	40	10%
2003	CFR	9/4/2003	$38.25	11/21/2003	$39.15	$43.07	$31.32	C.O	2/19/2004	W	60	6%
2003	CTCO	9/4/2003	$42.46	11/21/2003	$36.55	$40.21	$29.24	$41.25	2/10/2004	W	54	10%
2003	GB	9/4/2003	$39.50	11/21/2003	$38.40	$42.24	$30.72	$42.49	12/1/2003	W	6	10%

YEAR	TICKER SYMBOL	DATE ADDED	CLOSING PRICE	BUY DATE	OPENING PRICE	TARGET PRICE	STOP PRICE	HIGH PRICE	DATE	W/L	DAYS	P/L
2003	LXP	9/4/2003	$19.94	11/21/2003	$19.63	$21.59	$15.70	$21.80	2/2/2004	W	48	10%
2003	JBLU	9/23/2003	$26.78	12/11/2003	$17.90	$19.69	$14.32	C.O	3/9/2004	L	60	-13%
2003	RCII	9/25/2003	$32.32	12/15/2003	$32.42	$35.66	$25.94	C.O	3/11/2004	L	60	-3%
2003	HIW	10/7/2003	$25.77	12/26/2003	$25.49	$28.04	$20.39	C.O	3/23/2004	W	60	3%
2003	UMPQ	10/20/2003	$21.25	1/9/2004	$21.16	$23.28	$16.93	C.O	4/5/2004	L	60	-4%
2003	GTRC	10/31/2003	$32.57	1/23/2004	$33.02	$36.32	$26.42	$36.90	2/25/2004	W	23	10%
2003	MANT	10/31/2003	$24.75	1/23/2004	$22.69	$24.96	$18.15	C.O	4/19/2004	L	60	-2%
2003	SMG	10/31/2003	$24.83	1/23/2004	$25.08	$27.59	$20.06	$27.84	1/28/2004	W	4	10%
2003	RJF	11/12/2003	$17.89	2/4/2004	$16.71	$18.38	$13.37	C.O	4/29/2004	W	60	1%
2003	TRDO	12/30/2003	$22.20	3/22/2004	$19.73	$21.70	$15.78	C.O	6/16/2004	L	60	-15%
2004	NNN	2/10/2004	$19.26	4/30/2004	$16.70	$18.37	$13.36	C.O	7/27/2004	W	60	3%
2004	DAKT	2/12/2004	$13.54	5/4/2004	$10.77	$11.85	$8.62	$12.00	5/25/2004	W	16	10%
2004	ANN	2/26/2004	$30.47	5/17/2004	$26.77	$29.45	$21.42	$29.50	6/9/2004	W	17	10%
2004	HAR	2/26/2004	$76.90	5/17/2004	$70.54	$77.59	$56.43	$77.80	5/27/2004	W	9	10%
2004	JEF	2/26/2004	$18.50	5/17/2004	$15.93	$17.52	$12.74	C.O	8/11/2004	L	60	-3%
2004	RGS	2/26/2004	$43.29	5/17/2004	$41.10	$45.21	$32.88	$45.25	6/15/2004	W	20	10%
2004	MMSI	3/15/2004	$22.59	6/3/2004	$14.51	$15.96	$11.61	$16.18	6/29/2004	W	18	10%
2004	HW	3/29/2004	$24.55	6/18/2004	$24.95	$27.45	$19.96	$27.90	7/30/2004	W	30	10%
2004	ETFC	3/31/2004	$13.35	6/22/2004	$10.74	$11.81	$8.59	$12.70	8/19/2004	W	42	10%
2004	RYL	3/31/2004	$44.42	6/22/2004	$38.10	$41.91	$30.48	$43.13	8/17/2004	W	40	10%
2004	STSA	3/31/2004	$24.50	6/22/2004	$20.65	$22.72	$16.52	$22.82	9/3/2004	W	53	10%
2004	ACS	4/1/2004	$52.90	6/23/2004	$50.88	$55.97	$40.70	$56.92	9/10/2004	W	56	10%
2004	BLTI	4/1/2004	$18.01	6/23/2004	$14.92	$16.41	$11.94	S.O	7/19/2004	L	18	-20%
2004	MGAM	4/22/2004	$25.57	7/14/2004	$26.53	$29.18	$21.22	S.O	7/30/2004	L	13	-20%
2004	MYL	4/22/2004	$24.33	7/14/2004	$19.59	$21.55	$15.67	S.O	7/26/2004	L	9	-20%
2004	PSUN	4/22/2004	$23.06	7/14/2004	$19.58	$21.54	$15.66	$21.73	9/13/2004	W	43	10%
2004	HIBB	4/27/2004	$17.18	7/19/2004	$14.90	$16.39	$11.92	S.O	7/21/2004	L	3	-20%
2004	PXP	5/14/2004	$19.73	8/5/2004	$20.35	$22.39	$16.28	$22.88	9/20/2004	W	32	10%
2004	ROV	5/18/2004	$27.50	8/9/2004	$23.75	$26.13	$19.00	$26.46	9/17/2004	W	29	10%
2004	EPR	6/3/2004	$35.30	8/24/2004	$36.20	$39.82	$28.96	$39.97	10/27/2004	W	46	10%

YEAR	TICKER SYMBOL	DATE ADDED	CLOSING PRICE	BUY DATE	OPENING PRICE	TARGET PRICE	STOP PRICE	HIGH PRICE	DATE	W/L	DAYS	P/L
2004	UTSI	6/3/2004	$30.76	8/24/2004	$16.39	$18.03	$13.11	S.O	9/20/2004	L	19	-20%
2004	SAFM	6/17/2004	$52.46	9/7/2004	$34.40	$37.84	$27.52	$37.84	11/30/2004	W	60	10%
2004	LABS	6/24/2004	$31.77	9/14/2004	$28.63	$31.49	$22.90	$32.76	11/4/2004	W	38	10%
2004	ADS	6/30/2004	$42.25	9/20/2004	$39.75	$43.73	$31.80	$44.66	10/18/2004	W	21	10%
2004	DGIN	6/30/2004	$20.56	9/20/2004	$13.97	$15.37	$11.18	$15.73	10/22/2004	W	25	10%
2004	ARO	7/1/2004	$19.18	9/24/2004	$18.83	$20.71	$15.06	$20.74	10/19/2004	W	18	10%
2004	SSS	7/8/2004	$40.33	9/27/2004	$38.63	$42.49	$30.90	$42.74	11/15/2004	W	36	10%
2004	APSG	7/22/2004	$35.45	10/11/2004	$32.70	$35.97	$26.16	$36.66	11/12/2004	W	25	10%
2004	PVTB	7/22/2004	$28.57	10/11/2004	$28.05	$30.86	$22.44	$31.18	10/19/2004	W	7	10%
2004	BDY	7/23/2004	$25.01	10/12/2004	$19.08	$20.99	$15.26	S.O	10/22/2004	L	9	-20%
2004	ACO	7/30/2004	$20.10	10/19/2004	$17.60	$19.36	$14.08	$19.41	11/12/2004	W	19	10%
2004	FSH	8/2/2004	$59.60	10/20/2004	$53.50	$58.85	$42.80	$59.50	12/13/2004	W	38	10%
2004	IVGN	9/20/2004	$58.06	12/8/2004	$60.53	$66.58	$48.42	$67.32	12/13/2004	W	4	10%
2004	GTIV	9/28/2004	$16.25	12/16/2004	$16.25	$17.88	$13.00	C.O	3/14/2005	W	60	2%
2004	PETD	9/28/2004	$43.63	12/16/2004	$38.80	$42.68	$31.04	$43.54	2/14/2005	W	41	10%
2004	APH	9/30/2004	$17.13	12/20/2004	$17.86	$19.65	$14.29	$19.75	1/31/2005	W	29	10%
2004	AMED	10/22/2004	$23.02	1/12/2005	$20.26	$22.29	$16.21	$22.50	1/18/2005	W	4	10%
2004	WOOF	10/22/2004	$21.81	1/12/2005	$19.19	$21.11	$15.35	$21.21	3/29/2005	W	52	10%
2004	PKY	10/29/2004	$50.78	1/20/2005	$48.25	$53.08	$38.60	C.O	4/15/2005	L	60	-5%
2004	CRO	11/12/2004	$24.26	2/3/2005	$22.88	$25.17	$18.30	C.O	4/29/2005	W	60	1%
2004	SAH	11/30/2004	$24.83	2/18/2005	$23.87	$26.26	$19.10	C.O	5/16/2005	L	60	-14%
2004	TECH	11/30/2004	$37.40	2/18/2005	$34.44	$37.88	$27.55	$38.33	3/3/2005	W	9	10%
2004	SSI	11/30/2004	$18.14	2/18/2005	$17.45	$19.20	$13.96	C.O	5/16/2005	W	60	1%
2004	CRDN	12/7/2004	$33.81	2/28/2005	$29.95	$32.95	$23.96	S.O	3/21/2005	L	16	-20%
2004	ASN	12/17/2004	$39.00	3/10/2005	$34.70	$38.17	$27.76	C.O	6/3/2005	W	60	6%
2004	CBSS	12/17/2004	$47.45	3/10/2005	$46.71	$51.38	$37.37	C.O	6/3/2005	L	60	-5%
2004	NWS	12/17/2004	$18.83	3/10/2005	$17.60	$19.36	$14.08	C.O	6/3/2005	L	60	-5%
2005	PVA	2/22/2005	$23.56	5/12/2005	$21.09	$23.20	$16.87	$23.27	6/23/2005	W	30	10%
2005	MATK	3/1/2005	$68.70	5/19/2005	$41.17	$45.29	$32.94	$46.23	7/15/2005	W	40	10%
2005	FFIV	3/11/2005	$28.93	6/1/2005	$25.50	$28.05	$20.40	S.O	7/21/2005	L	36	-20%

137

YEAR	TICKER SYMBOL	DATE ADDED	CLOSING PRICE	BUY DATE	OPENING PRICE	TARGET PRICE	STOP PRICE	HIGH PRICE	DATE	W/L	DAYS	P/L
2005	FINL	3/11/2005	$22.13	6/1/2005	$19.81	$21.79	$15.85	C.O	8/24/2005	L	60	-19%
2005	YRCW	3/11/2005	$62.49	6/1/2005	$52.82	$58.10	$42.26	C.O	8/24/2005	L	60	-10%
2005	TRBS	4/5/2005	$31.25	6/23/2005	$29.22	$32.14	$23.38	$32.43	7/11/2005	W	12	10%
2005	IPMT	4/15/2005	$41.48	7/6/2005	$36.51	$40.16	$29.21	$40.50	8/8/2005	W	24	10%
2005	AKR	5/25/2005	$16.94	8/15/2005	$17.60	$19.36	$14.08	$19.43	11/3/2005	W	58	10%
2005	WDC	6/13/2005	$15.65	8/31/2005	$13.43	$14.77	$10.74	$14.85	9/7/2005	W	5	10%
2005	STZ	7/1/2005	$29.90	9/21/2005	$26.50	$29.15	$21.20	S.O	10/13/2005	L	17	-20%
2005	ISRG	7/29/2005	$69.40	10/18/2005	$67.50	$74.25	$54.00	$92.64	10/26/2005	W	7	10%
2005	USNA	8/2/2005	$51.65	10/20/2005	$43.51	$47.86	$34.81	C.O	1/17/2006	L	60	-8%
2005	RRGB	8/9/2005	$59.44	10/27/2005	$46.15	$50.77	$36.92	$52.67	11/4/2005	W	7	10%
2005	MHO	8/18/2005	$56.22	11/7/2005	$45.67	$50.24	$36.54	S.O	1/23/2006	L	52	-20%
2005	PSA	8/18/2005	$66.24	11/7/2005	$66.12	$72.73	$52.90	$72.79	1/9/2006	W	43	10%
2005	ASVI	8/29/2005	$23.85	11/16/2005	$22.93	$25.22	$18.34	$25.79	11/21/2005	W	4	10%
2005	TKR	8/29/2005	$28.54	11/16/2005	$29.75	$32.73	$23.80	$32.73	12/7/2005	W	15	10%
2005	JOYG	8/31/2005	$32.05	11/18/2005	$31.55	$34.71	$25.24	$35.58	11/29/2005	W	7	10%
2005	MCY	8/31/2005	$58.73	11/18/2005	$59.05	$64.96	$47.24	C.O	2/15/2006	L	60	-4%
2005	PRSP	9/27/2005	$30.10	12/15/2005	$30.54	$33.59	$24.43	C.O	3/14/2006	L	60	-3%
2005	UFCS	9/30/2005	$45.11	12/20/2005	$41.14	$45.25	$32.91	S.O	3/7/2006	L	52	-20%
2005	LEN	10/3/2005	$61.70	12/21/2005	$62.15	$68.37	$49.72	C.O	3/20/2006	L	60	-5%
2005	GME	10/7/2005	$15.35	12/28/2005	$15.55	$17.11	$12.44	$19.23	1/5/2006	W	6	10%
2005	LSCP	10/7/2005	$28.20	12/28/2005	$21.95	$24.15	$17.56	$27.40	1/5/2006	W	6	10%
2005	PDCO	10/10/2005	$39.96	12/29/2005	$33.81	$37.19	$27.05	C.O	3/27/2006	W	60	4%
2005	HUBG	10/14/2005	$17.14	1/5/2006	$17.77	$19.55	$14.22	$19.87	1/23/2006	W	12	10%
2005	CNXS	10/20/2005	$26.05	1/11/2006	$23.15	$25.47	$18.52	$25.69	1/25/2006	W	10	10%
2005	GVHR	10/26/2005	$26.73	1/18/2006	$24.32	$26.75	$19.46	$27.16	1/27/2006	W	8	10%
2005	CATY	10/27/2005	$38.29	1/19/2006	$36.47	$40.12	$29.18	C.O	4/13/2006	W	60	3%
2005	MSA	10/27/2005	$41.50	1/19/2006	$40.60	$44.66	$32.48	C.O	4/13/2006	W	60	1%
2005	INSP	11/15/2005	$19.47	2/7/2006	$17.60	$19.36	$14.08	$20.08	3/16/2006	W	27	10%
2005	AMZN	11/18/2005	$47.98	2/10/2006	$37.98	$41.78	$30.38	C.O	5/8/2006	L	60	-9%
2005	QSII	11/22/2005	$43.53	2/14/2006	$33.24	$36.56	$26.59	$37.10	2/17/2006	W	4	10%

138

Chapter 10: Track Records and Statistics

YEAR	TICKER SYMBOL	DATE ADDED	CLOSING PRICE	BUY DATE	OPENING PRICE	TARGET PRICE	STOP PRICE	HIGH PRICE	DATE	W/L	DAYS	P/L
2005	GNW	12/1/2005	$34.93	2/23/2006	$33.45	$36.80	$26.76	C.O	5/18/2006	L	60	-4%
2005	GBCI	12/2/2005	$22.18	2/24/2006	$20.95	$23.05	$16.76	C.O	5/19/2006	L	60	-7%
2005	SJI	12/2/2005	$29.44	2/24/2006	$29.40	$32.34	$23.52	C.O	5/19/2006	L	60	-10%
2005	KWK	12/5/2005	$22.00	2/27/2006	$18.84	$20.72	$15.07	$21.38	4/18/2006	W	36	10%
2005	NCI	12/9/2005	$23.30	3/3/2006	$18.98	$20.88	$15.18	$21.17	3/29/2006	W	19	10%
2005	NVTL	12/12/2005	$13.97	3/6/2006	$8.37	$9.21	$6.70	$9.34	3/29/2006	W	18	10%
2005	LUFK	12/13/2005	$55.09	3/7/2006	$50.63	$55.69	$40.50	$55.70	3/28/2006	W	16	10%
2005	FFFL	12/15/2005	$34.12	3/9/2006	$32.47	$35.72	$25.98	C.O	6/2/2006	W	60	2%
2005	NSS	12/28/2005	$42.44	3/21/2006	$41.45	$45.60	$33.16	$45.96	3/28/2006	W	6	10%
2005	BCSI	12/29/2005	$23.12	3/22/2006	$10.13	$11.14	$8.10	$11.23	4/5/2006	W	11	10%
2005	AFFX	12/30/2005	$47.75	3/23/2006	$30.97	$34.07	$24.78	$35.62	4/19/2006	W	19	10%
2005	WFMI	12/30/2005	$77.39	3/23/2006	$64.15	$70.57	$51.32	$74.00	4/11/2006	W	14	10%
2006	PSTI	1/6/2006	$24.89	3/29/2006	$25.97	$28.57	$20.78	$29.25	5/5/2006	W	27	10%
2006	PPDI	1/25/2006	$33.00	4/17/2006	$32.85	$36.14	$26.28	$41.17	4/18/2006	W	2	10%
2006	UTI	1/25/2006	$35.77	4/17/2006	$23.88	$26.27	$19.10	$26.50	5/10/2006	W	18	10%
2006	HAFC	1/30/2006	$19.44	4/20/2006	$17.95	$19.75	$14.36	$19.80	5/1/2006	W	8	10%
2006	HARB	1/31/2006	$38.95	4/21/2006	$38.12	$41.93	$30.50	$44.50	7/11/2006	W	56	10%
2006	VRSN	1/31/2006	$23.75	4/21/2006	$24.25	$26.68	$19.40	C.O	7/17/2006	L	60	-13%
2006	LTC	2/14/2006	$22.03	5/5/2006	$22.06	$24.27	$17.65	C.O	7/31/2006	L	60	0%
2006	BRL	2/24/2006	$66.80	5/16/2006	$50.29	$55.32	$40.23	C.O	8/9/2006	W	60	3%
2006	FNFG	2/24/2006	$14.64	5/16/2006	$13.94	$15.33	$11.15	C.O	8/9/2006	W	60	2%
2006	CHK	3/2/2006	$31.70	5/22/2006	$29.00	$31.90	$23.20	$32.10	7/27/2006	W	47	10%
2006	VTIV	3/9/2006	$29.13	5/30/2006	$29.90	$32.89	$23.92	C.O	8/22/2006	W	60	2%
2006	NWRE	3/13/2006	$25.15	6/1/2006	$20.66	$22.73	$16.53	S.O	6/29/2006	L	21	-20%
2006	TUES	3/29/2006	$22.92	6/19/2006	$14.01	$15.41	$11.21	C.O	9/12/2006	L	60	-6%
2006	MATR	3/30/2006	$38.01	6/20/2006	$21.32	$23.45	$17.06	$24.69	7/19/2006	W	21	10%
2006	BXP	3/31/2006	$93.25	6/21/2006	$87.36	$96.10	$69.89	$96.30	7/26/2006	W	25	10%
2006	FCF	3/31/2006	$14.66	6/21/2006	$12.47	$13.72	$9.98	C.O	9/14/2006	W	60	3%
2006	GOOG	3/31/2006	$390.00	6/21/2006	$391.06	$430.17	$312.85	C.O	9/14/2006	W	60	3%
2006	KIM	4/3/2006	$39.50	6/22/2006	$35.73	$39.30	$28.58	$39.72	7/28/2006	W	26	10%

139

YEAR	TICKER SYMBOL	DATE ADDED	CLOSING PRICE	BUY DATE	OPENING PRICE	TARGET PRICE	STOP PRICE	HIGH PRICE	DATE	W/L	DAYS	P/L
2006	LOJN	4/4/2006	$23.77	6/23/2006	$17.52	$19.27	$14.02	$19.78	8/7/2006	W	31	10%
2006	TRAD	4/5/2006	$14.60	6/26/2006	$12.70	$13.97	$10.16	$14.22	7/20/2006	W	18	10%
2006	UNTD	4/13/2006	$13.19	7/5/2006	$11.84	$13.02	$9.47	C.O	9/27/2006	W	60	2%
2006	SGMS	4/19/2006	$37.84	7/10/2006	$35.60	$39.16	$28.48	S.O	8/23/2006	L	33	-20%
2006	SNDK	4/19/2006	$63.77	7/10/2006	$47.65	$52.42	$38.12	S.O	7/18/2006	L	7	-20%
2006	WIBC	4/28/2006	$18.24	7/19/2006	$17.94	$19.73	$14.35	$19.97	8/14/2006	W	19	10%
2006	DECK	5/1/2006	$42.49	7/20/2006	$36.50	$40.15	$29.20	$43.83	7/28/2006	W	7	10%
2006	STL	5/3/2006	$20.85	7/24/2006	$18.80	$20.68	$15.04	$21.00	9/11/2006	W	35	10%
2006	ROIAK	5/5/2006	$7.90	7/26/2006	$6.90	$7.59	$5.52	C.O	10/18/2006	L	60	-6%
2006	FINB	6/1/2006	$27.19	8/21/2006	$24.52	$26.97	$19.62	$28.32	10/23/2006	W	45	10%
2006	CBH	6/5/2006	$39.56	8/23/2006	$33.25	$36.58	$26.60	$37.59	9/18/2006	W	18	10%
2006	RS	6/5/2006	$39.58	8/23/2006	$32.45	$35.70	$25.96	$35.99	10/18/2006	W	40	10%
2006	STMP	6/5/2006	$33.20	8/23/2006	$20.05	$22.06	$16.04	S.O	10/20/2006	L	42	-20%
2006	PALM	6/8/2006	$9.53	8/28/2006	$7.70	$8.47	$6.16	$8.65	10/12/2006	W	33	10%
2006	PETS	6/12/2006	$13.70	8/30/2006	$12.85	$14.14	$10.28	S.O	9/6/2006	L	5	-20%
2006	RCRC	6/29/2006	$38.78	9/19/2006	$34.72	$38.19	$27.78	$40.95	10/13/2006	W	19	10%
2006	PSB	7/27/2006	$60.45	10/16/2006	$61.65	$67.82	$49.32	$67.90	11/16/2006	W	24	10%
2006	KEYS	8/1/2006	$41.74	10/19/2006	$41.77	$45.95	$33.42	S.O	12/7/2006	L	35	-20%
2006	MAA	8/22/2006	$59.70	11/9/2006	$60.20	$66.22	$48.16	C.O	2/7/2007	L	60	0%
2006	PSYS	9/14/2006	$35.40	12/4/2006	$36.94	$40.63	$29.55	$42.88	2/16/2007	W	51	10%
2006	VIVO	9/18/2006	$16.13	12/6/2006	$16.28	$17.91	$13.02	$18.07	1/11/2007	W	24	10%
2006	STRA	10/31/2006	$113.12	1/24/2007	$109.75	$120.73	$87.80	$125.30	2/15/2007	W	17	10%
2006	CELG	11/3/2006	$51.65	1/29/2007	$53.38	$58.72	$42.70	$59.10	4/9/2007	W	49	10%
2006	IVAC	11/6/2006	$23.35	1/30/2007	$22.80	$25.08	$18.24	$29.20	2/7/2007	W	7	10%
2006	FIS	11/9/2006	$23.03	2/2/2007	$23.71	$26.08	$18.97	$26.18	2/14/2007	W	9	10%
2006	JNC	11/9/2006	$51.85	2/2/2007	$50.98	$56.08	$40.78	C.O	4/27/2007	W	60	2%
2006	VMSI	11/10/2006	$43.63	2/5/2007	$40.32	$44.35	$32.26	$46.10	4/13/2007	W	48	10%
2006	CACB	11/29/2006	$30.94	2/22/2007	$27.32	$30.05	$21.86	S.O	4/30/2007	L	47	-20%
2006	STR	11/30/2006	$43.13	2/23/2007	$40.51	$44.56	$32.41	$44.76	3/21/2007	W	19	10%
2006	DIGE	12/1/2006	$51.06	2/23/2007	$47.89	$52.68	$38.31	S.O	3/20/2007	L	18	-20%

Chapter 10: Track Records and Statistics

YEAR	TICKER SYMBOL	DATE ADDED	CLOSING PRICE	BUY DATE	OPENING PRICE	TARGET PRICE	STOP PRICE	HIGH PRICE	DATE	W/L	DAYS	P/L
2006	CENT	12/6/2006	$17.87	3/1/2007	$13.85	$15.24	$11.08	$15.37	3/23/2007	W	17	10%
2006	CTCI	12/19/2006	$22.93	3/14/2007	$23.45	$25.80	$18.76	$25.94	4/2/2007	W	14	10%
2006	MTEX	12/19/2006	$15.53	3/14/2007	$14.34	$15.77	$11.47	$16.19	3/30/2007	W	13	10%
2006	TEX	12/19/2006	$65.67	3/14/2007	$66.69	$73.36	$53.35	$73.56	4/9/2007	W	18	10%
2006	FCFS	12/29/2006	$25.87	3/23/2007	$22.63	$24.89	$18.10	$25.08	4/18/2007	W	18	10%
2007	HOS	1/3/2007	$35.09	3/26/2007	$29.00	$31.90	$23.20	$32.00	4/26/2007	W	23	10%
2007	XEC	1/3/2007	$36.66	3/26/2007	$36.60	$40.26	$29.28	$40.30	4/30/2007	W	25	10%
2007	GPN	1/9/2007	$40.11	3/30/2007	$39.93	$43.92	$31.94	S.O	3/30/2007	L	1	-20%
2007	ROCK	1/9/2007	$23.92	3/30/2007	$22.84	$25.12	$18.27	C.O	6/25/2007	L	60	-7%
2007	TGIC	1/12/2007	$56.65	4/4/2007	$41.56	$45.72	$33.25	$46.10	4/26/2007	W	16	10%
2007	CORS	1/24/2007	$21.71	4/16/2007	$16.92	$18.61	$13.54	$18.74	5/23/2007	W	28	10%
2007	VPHM	1/25/2007	$16.06	4/17/2007	$15.43	$16.97	$12.34	C.O	7/11/2007	L	60	-6%
2007	CHRW	3/1/2007	$50.97	5/21/2007	$52.30	$57.53	$41.84	C.O	8/14/2007	L	60	-9%
2007	RUTH	3/7/2007	$21.35	5/25/2007	$18.85	$20.74	$15.08	S.O	8/1/2007	L	47	-20%
2007	ANF	3/28/2007	$76.19	6/18/2007	$78.01	$85.81	$62.41	C.O	9/11/2007	L	60	-1%
2007	BLKB	3/28/2007	$24.21	6/18/2007	$22.41	$24.65	$17.93	$25.00	8/7/2007	W	36	10%
2007	PVH	3/28/2007	$58.69	6/18/2007	$60.63	$66.69	$48.50	S.O	8/15/2007	L	42	-20%
2007	NVR	4/4/2007	$692.00	6/25/2007	$681.20	$749.32	$544.96	S.O	8/15/2007	L	37	-20%
2007	SMA	4/11/2007	$17.70	6/29/2007	$16.01	$17.61	$12.81	$18.18	8/17/2007	W	35	10%
2007	INFA	4/12/2007	$14.45	7/2/2007	$14.85	$16.34	$11.88	C.O	9/25/2007	W	60	5%
2007	KRG	4/13/2007	$21.11	7/3/2007	$19.23	$21.15	$15.38	S.O	7/30/2007	L	19	-20%
2007	LAD	4/18/2007	$28.27	7/9/2007	$24.66	$27.13	$19.73	S.O	7/30/2007	L	16	-20%
2007	CGI	4/20/2007	$33.47	7/11/2007	$34.47	$37.92	$27.58	S.O	8/3/2007	L	18	-20%
2007	MTRX	5/1/2007	$25.02	7/20/2007	$24.95	$27.45	$19.96	S.O	8/6/2007	L	12	-20%
2007	TXRH	5/8/2007	$15.54	7/27/2007	$12.86	$14.15	$10.29	C.O	10/19/2007	L	60	-13%
2007	KND	5/22/2007	$33.40	8/10/2007	$18.95	$20.85	$15.16	$20.99	10/30/2007	W	57	10%
2007	DRIV	5/31/2007	$51.42	8/20/2007	$44.14	$48.55	$35.31	$49.18	10/8/2007	W	35	10%
2007	ENDP	5/31/2007	$35.26	8/20/2007	$31.36	$34.50	$25.09	S.O	11/12/2007	L	60	-12%
2007	CHIC	6/4/2007	$29.26	8/22/2007	$18.39	$20.23	$14.71	S.O	9/27/2007	L	26	-20%
2007	SINT	6/5/2007	$32.46	8/23/2007	$30.20	$33.22	$24.16	C.O	11/15/2007	L	60	-10%

141

YEAR	TICKER SYMBOL	DATE ADDED	CLOSING PRICE	BUY DATE	OPENING PRICE	TARGET PRICE	STOP PRICE	HIGH PRICE	DATE	W/L	DAYS	P/L
2007	SSYS	6/14/2007	$24.44	9/4/2007	$25.41	$27.95	$20.33	$29.42	9/19/2007	W	12	10%
2007	VLCM	6/15/2007	$45.74	9/5/2007	$38.54	$42.39	$30.83	$42.39	9/27/2007	W	17	10%
2007	TTMI	6/20/2007	$12.87	9/10/2007	$11.45	$12.60	$9.16	$12.92	9/19/2007	W	8	10%
2007	TWGP	6/25/2007	$32.81	9/13/2007	$24.84	$27.32	$19.87	$28.11	10/2/2007	W	14	10%
2007	GGP	6/29/2007	$52.95	9/19/2007	$52.26	$57.49	$41.81	$57.80	10/10/2007	W	16	10%
2007	MFB	7/2/2007	$21.15	9/20/2007	$17.24	$18.96	$13.79	S.O	11/5/2007	L	33	-20%
2007	ACAS	7/6/2007	$46.97	9/25/2007	$40.87	$44.96	$32.70	$44.98	10/5/2007	W	9	10%
2007	BBG	7/6/2007	$38.30	9/25/2007	$38.50	$42.35	$30.80	$42.42	10/2/2007	W	6	10%
2007	AKAM	7/11/2007	$50.32	9/28/2007	$28.25	$31.08	$22.60	$31.66	10/2/2007	W	3	10%
2007	WRNC	7/17/2007	$40.89	10/4/2007	$39.46	$43.41	$31.57	$44.94	10/8/2007	W	3	10%
2007	MDTH	7/25/2007	$32.25	10/12/2007	$28.98	$31.88	$23.18	S.O	11/14/2007	L	24	-20%
2007	IEX	8/1/2007	$37.19	10/19/2007	$37.36	$41.10	$29.89	C.O	1/15/2008	L	60	-17%
2007	SNX	8/2/2007	$20.68	10/22/2007	$21.58	$23.74	$17.26	$23.81	1/14/2008	W	58	10%
2007	PRFT	8/13/2007	$23.07	10/31/2007	$18.58	$20.44	$14.86	S.O	12/5/2007	L	25	-20%
2007	LUK	8/24/2007	$44.48	11/13/2007	$43.59	$47.95	$34.87	$48.32	12/5/2007	W	16	10%
2007	LTM	8/24/2007	$55.50	11/13/2007	$57.46	$63.21	$45.97	S.O	12/20/2007	L	27	-20%
2007	MCHP	9/7/2007	$37.53	11/27/2007	$27.58	$30.34	$22.06	$30.75	12/6/2007	W	8	10%
2007	JLL	9/7/2007	$102.25	11/27/2007	$72.86	$80.15	$58.29	$81.14	11/28/2007	W	2	10%
2007	TSO	9/26/2007	$49.70	12/14/2007	$45.11	$49.62	$36.09	$50.00	12/17/2007	W	2	10%
2007	DRE	9/28/2007	$33.81	12/18/2007	$24.94	$27.43	$19.95	C.O	3/14/2008	L	60	-13%
2007	SWSI	9/28/2007	$22.73	12/18/2007	$19.71	$21.68	$15.77	$21.86	12/21/2007	W	4	10%
2007	SAM	9/28/2007	$48.66	12/18/2007	$34.50	$37.95	$27.60	$38.65	12/21/2007	W	4	10%
2007	EXPE	10/1/2007	$33.44	12/19/2007	$32.67	$35.94	$26.14	S.O	1/15/2008	L	18	-20%
2007	CPO	10/1/2007	$46.98	12/19/2007	$36.95	$40.65	$29.56	C.O	3/17/2008	W	60	3%
2007	BWLD	10/1/2007	$38.13	12/19/2007	$27.30	$30.03	$21.84	S.O	1/3/2008	L	10	-20%
2007	LAMR	10/5/2007	$55.41	12/26/2007	$48.23	$53.05	$38.58	S.O	2/27/2008	L	43	-20%
2007	EXPD	10/9/2007	$51.86	12/28/2007	$45.57	$50.13	$36.46	C.O	3/26/2008	L	60	-3%
2007	BAS	10/18/2007	$20.88	1/9/2008	$19.70	$21.67	$15.76	$21.94	2/13/2008	W	25	10%
2007	NYX	10/24/2007	$90.00	1/15/2008	$83.62	$91.98	$66.90	S.O	1/22/2008	L	5	-20%
2007	JEC	10/25/2007	$83.61	1/16/2008	$79.57	$87.53	$63.66	C.O	4/11/2008	L	60	-3%

Tailwind Trading System

Chapter 10: Track Records and Statistics

YEAR	TICKER SYMBOL	DATE ADDED	CLOSING PRICE	BUY DATE	OPENING PRICE	TARGET PRICE	STOP PRICE	HIGH PRICE	DATE	W/L	DAYS	P/L
2007	CMG	10/26/2007	$133.95	1/17/2008	$122.29	$134.52	$97.83	$135.40	1/24/2008	W	5	10%
2007	SPAR	11/1/2007	$13.50	1/24/2008	$8.54	$9.39	$6.83	$9.45	2/1/2008	W	7	10%
2007	KCI	11/6/2007	$62.50	1/29/2008	$50.25	$55.28	$40.20	S.O	4/15/2008	L	54	-20%
2007	POM	11/8/2007	$25.80	1/31/2008	$25.12	$27.63	$20.10	C.O	4/25/2008	L	60	0%
2007	EGN	11/8/2007	$62.99	1/31/2008	$61.29	$67.42	$49.03	$67.49	4/9/2008	W	48	10%
2007	DRH	11/8/2007	$18.02	1/31/2008	$13.24	$14.56	$10.59	C.O	4/25/2008	L	60	-2%
2007	HCN	11/8/2007	$43.69	1/31/2008	$42.07	$46.28	$33.66	$46.45	3/25/2008	W	37	10%
2007	O	11/13/2007	$30.45	2/5/2008	$24.50	$26.95	$19.60	$27.05	3/19/2008	W	31	10%
2007	MTW	11/15/2007	$39.50	2/7/2008	$37.00	$40.70	$29.60	$41.80	2/21/2008	W	10	10%
2007	WXS	11/15/2007	$40.00	2/7/2008	$31.29	$34.42	$25.03	$34.58	4/16/2008	W	48	10%
2007	WAB	11/16/2007	$35.11	2/8/2008	$33.49	$36.84	$26.79	$37.09	2/26/2008	W	12	10%
2007	BRE	11/19/2007	$47.21	2/11/2008	$41.37	$45.51	$33.10	$45.76	2/26/2008	W	11	10%
2007	COLB	11/20/2007	$30.13	2/12/2008	$24.28	$26.71	$19.42	$27.25	4/29/2008	W	54	10%
2007	ARE	12/3/2007	$99.20	2/25/2008	$94.02	$103.42	$75.22	$103.58	4/18/2008	W	39	10%
2007	KSU	12/6/2007	$36.54	2/28/2008	$37.41	$41.15	$29.93	$41.55	3/25/2008	W	18	10%
2007	BMR	12/6/2007	$24.14	2/28/2008	$21.12	$23.23	$16.90	$23.24	3/3/2008	W	3	10%
2007	ANDE	12/14/2007	$42.83	3/7/2008	$43.30	$47.63	$34.64	C.O	6/2/2008	L	60	-5%
2007	SLXP	12/18/2007	$11.56	3/11/2008	$5.76	$6.34	$4.61	$6.42	3/17/2008	W	5	10%
2007	FRT	12/20/2007	$81.25	3/13/2008	$70.50	$77.55	$56.40	$77.84	3/18/2008	W	4	10%
2007	FDRY	12/27/2007	$18.19	3/19/2008	$11.59	$12.75	$9.27	$13.09	4/25/2008	W	27	10%
2007	WPO	12/28/2007	$801.50	3/20/2008	$657.50	$723.25	$526.00	C.O	6/13/2008	L	60	-10%
2007	NAVG	12/31/2007	$65.00	3/24/2008	$53.77	$59.15	$43.02	C.O	6/16/2008	L	60	-1%
2008	HMSY	1/22/2008	$34.40	4/11/2008	$28.12	$30.93	$22.50	S.O	4/18/2008	L	6	-20%
2008	CXW	1/28/2008	$26.18	4/17/2008	$26.73	$29.40	$21.38	C.O	7/11/2008	W	60	1%
2008	NEU	2/12/2008	$62.12	5/2/2008	$63.39	$69.73	$50.71	$70.29	5/15/2008	W	10	10%
2008	NPBC	2/21/2008	$17.13	5/12/2008	$16.55	$18.21	$13.24	S.O	7/1/2008	L	36	-20%
2008	PEI	3/5/2008	$25.56	5/23/2008	$26.53	$29.18	$21.22	S.O	7/7/2008	L	30	-20%
2008	AIRM	3/25/2008	$48.49	6/12/2008	$36.00	$39.60	$28.80	S.O	6/25/2008	L	10	-20%
2008	NTRI	4/15/2008	$19.83	7/3/2008	$13.42	$14.76	$10.74	$15.11	7/11/2008	W	6	10%
2008	AMG	4/21/2008	$98.60	7/10/2008	$82.74	$91.01	$66.19	$93.98	7/23/2008	W	10	10%

143

Tailwind Trading System

Chapter 10: Track Records and Statistics

YEAR	TICKER SYMBOL	DATE ADDED	CLOSING PRICE	BUY DATE	OPENING PRICE	TARGET PRICE	STOP PRICE	HIGH PRICE	DATE	W/L	DAYS	P/L
2008	HS	5/7/2008	$17.73	7/28/2008	$17.95	$19.75	$14.36	$19.91	7/30/2008	W	3	10%
2008	DWA	5/8/2008	$29.98	7/29/2008	$31.00	$34.10	$24.80	S.O	10/9/2008	L	52	-20%
2008	UA	5/15/2008	$36.40	8/5/2008	$31.22	$34.34	$24.98	$36.50	8/8/2008	W	4	10%
2008	NFP	5/16/2008	$24.85	8/6/2008	$19.89	$21.88	$15.91	S.O	8/6/2008	L	1	-20%
2008	ZEUS	5/27/2008	$61.74	8/14/2008	$50.96	$56.06	$40.77	S.O	9/4/2008	L	15	-20%
2008	DAR	5/29/2008	$16.25	8/18/2008	$13.30	$14.63	$10.64	S.O	9/18/2008	L	23	-20%
2008	ISRG	5/30/2008	$293.59	8/19/2008	$292.86	$322.15	$234.29	S.O	9/30/2008	L	30	-20%
2008	SGR	5/30/2008	$61.00	8/19/2008	$48.83	$53.71	$39.06	S.O	9/8/2008	L	14	-20%
2008	SWN	6/5/2008	$46.04	8/25/2008	$38.07	$41.88	$30.46	S.O	9/9/2008	L	11	-20%
2008	CBSH	6/5/2008	$43.82	8/25/2008	$44.02	$48.42	$35.22	$48.62	9/16/2008	W	16	10%
2008	COG	6/20/2008	$65.40	9/10/2008	$35.27	$38.80	$28.22	$39.46	9/12/2008	W	3	10%
2008	MEE	6/20/2008	$89.36	9/10/2008	$39.50	$43.45	$31.60	$43.78	9/10/2008	W	1	10%
2008	FLIR	6/20/2008	$39.20	9/10/2008	$34.13	$37.54	$27.30	$38.99	9/19/2008	W	8	10%
2008	TRMB	6/20/2008	$36.72	9/10/2008	$29.45	$32.40	$23.56	$32.97	9/19/2008	W	8	10%
2008	AKS	6/30/2008	$69.00	9/18/2008	$27.98	$30.78	$22.38	$32.37	9/19/2008	W	2	10%
2008	HLX	7/9/2008	$36.75	9/26/2008	$25.93	$28.52	$20.74	S.O	10/2/2008	L	5	-20%
2008	BABY	7/15/2008	$21.26	10/2/2008	$22.18	$24.40	$17.74	S.O	10/10/2008	L	7	-20%
2008	MA	7/17/2008	$286.00	10/6/2008	$151.16	$166.28	$120.93	$170.90	10/6/2008	W	1	10%
2008	DVA	7/30/2008	$56.00	10/17/2008	$48.96	$53.86	$39.17	$54.27	10/30/2008	W	10	10%
2008	ECLP	7/31/2008	$22.05	10/20/2008	$16.58	$18.24	$13.26	S.O	11/6/2008	L	14	-20%
2008	ANSS	7/31/2008	$45.88	10/20/2008	$29.47	$32.42	$23.58	S.O	10/24/2008	L	5	-20%
2008	PCLN	8/1/2008	$116.66	10/21/2008	$59.35	$65.29	$47.48	S.O	10/24/2008	L	4	-20%
2008	CDR	8/4/2008	$12.46	10/22/2008	$8.77	$9.65	$7.02	S.O	11/13/2008	L	17	-20%
2008	SCL	8/19/2008	$59.92	11/6/2008	$35.00	$38.50	$28.00	$39.07	11/25/2008	W	14	10%
2008	BKE	8/19/2008	$32.80	11/6/2008	$24.37	$26.81	$19.50	S.O	11/13/2008	L	6	-20%
2008	IVZ	8/20/2008	$25.25	11/7/2008	$13.08	$14.39	$10.46	$14.60	11/10/2008	W	2	10%
2008	CRM	9/12/2008	$57.20	12/2/2008	$26.20	$28.82	$20.96	$29.12	12/2/2008	W	1	10%
2008	SF	9/12/2008	$41.92	12/2/2008	$39.59	$43.55	$31.67	$45.24	12/8/2008	W	5	10%
2008	UTHR	9/12/2008	$113.32	12/2/2008	$52.07	$57.28	$41.66	$58.40	12/9/2008	W	6	10%
2008	FAST	9/12/2008	$53.57	12/2/2008	$34.38	$37.82	$27.50	$37.86	2/10/2009	W	48	10%

144

Chapter 10: Track Records and Statistics

YEAR	TICKER SYMBOL	DATE ADDED	CLOSING PRICE	BUY DATE	OPENING PRICE	TARGET PRICE	STOP PRICE	HIGH PRICE	DATE	W/L	DAYS	P/L
2008	ESS	9/12/2008	$117.12	12/2/2008	$71.11	$78.22	$56.89	$79.28	12/2/2008	W	1	10%
2008	JCG	9/18/2008	$32.32	12/8/2008	$12.79	$14.07	$10.23	$14.30	12/8/2008	W	1	10%
2008	HRS	9/19/2008	$48.01	12/9/2008	$34.50	$37.95	$27.60	$38.01	12/19/2008	W	9	10%
2008	GEF	9/19/2008	$71.01	12/9/2008	$28.46	$31.31	$22.77	$31.64	12/10/2008	W	2	10%
2008	BXS	9/23/2008	$29.50	12/11/2008	$20.34	$22.37	$16.27	$22.40	12/30/2008	W	13	10%
2008	PXD	9/23/2008	$56.50	12/11/2008	$18.25	$20.08	$14.60	S.O	12/23/2008	L	9	-20%
2008	APH	9/29/2008	$40.27	12/17/2008	$22.61	$24.87	$18.09	$25.57	1/2/2009	W	11	10%
2008	UBA	9/29/2008	$18.60	12/17/2008	$16.25	$17.88	$13.00	S.O	2/17/2009	L	41	-20%
2008	OII	9/29/2008	$53.23	12/17/2008	$27.14	$29.85	$21.71	$30.56	1/2/2009	W	11	10%
2008	HPY	10/1/2008	$27.04	12/19/2008	$17.03	$18.73	$13.62	$18.93	1/6/2009	W	11	10%
2008	FLS	10/1/2008	$87.50	12/19/2008	$50.97	$56.07	$40.78	$56.35	1/5/2009	W	10	10%
2008	UGI	10/1/2008	$26.35	12/19/2008	$23.98	$26.38	$19.18	$26.48	1/28/2009	W	26	10%
2008	TLEO	10/1/2008	$20.26	12/19/2008	$7.61	$8.37	$6.09	$8.45	1/8/2009	W	13	10%
2008	MWIV	10/2/2008	$41.50	12/22/2008	$23.66	$26.03	$18.93	$27.74	12/31/2008	W	7	10%
2008	TKLC	10/3/2008	$13.66	12/23/2008	$13.12	$14.43	$10.50	$14.43	2/11/2009	W	34	10%
2008	DPS	10/6/2008	$24.90	12/24/2008	$16.96	$18.66	$13.57	S.O	3/2/2009	L	45	-20%
2008	CCC	10/10/2008	$16.70	12/31/2008	$14.63	$16.09	$11.70	$16.39	1/2/2009	W	2	10%
2008	PPS	10/15/2008	$22.43	1/6/2009	$16.23	$17.85	$12.98	S.O	1/15/2009	L	8	-20%
2008	NDAQ	10/21/2008	$33.09	1/12/2009	$21.87	$24.06	$17.50	$25.07	2/6/2009	W	19	10%
2008	CRK	10/21/2008	$43.35	1/12/2009	$43.55	$47.91	$34.84	S.O	2/18/2009	L	26	-20%
2008	ISYS	10/21/2008	$21.11	1/12/2009	$13.06	$14.37	$10.45	S.O	2/2/2009	L	15	-20%
2008	CRVL	10/27/2008	$24.46	1/16/2009	$19.19	$21.11	$15.35	$21.36	2/6/2009	W	15	10%
2008	CLH	10/27/2008	$57.76	1/16/2009	$53.94	$59.33	$43.15	S.O	3/9/2009	L	35	-20%
2008	WEC	10/30/2008	$43.80	1/22/2009	$42.13	$46.34	$33.70	$46.35	1/28/2009	W	5	10%
2008	UNT	10/30/2008	$35.95	1/22/2009	$25.81	$28.39	$20.65	S.O	2/27/2009	L	26	-20%
2008	CALM	10/30/2008	$28.59	1/22/2009	$27.31	$30.04	$21.85	S.O	3/2/2009	L	27	-20%
2008	CRI	10/31/2008	$21.24	1/23/2009	$16.63	$18.29	$13.30	$18.42	1/28/2009	W	4	10%
2008	FULT	11/10/2008	$11.00	2/2/2009	$7.01	$7.71	$5.61	$7.76	2/9/2009	W	6	10%
2008	PBCT	11/12/2008	$17.94	2/4/2009	$16.96	$18.66	$13.57	C.O	4/30/2009	L	60	-8%
2008	WYNN	11/13/2008	$44.76	2/5/2009	$26.00	$28.60	$20.80	$29.20	2/5/2009	W	1	10%

145

Tailwind Trading System

Chapter 10: Track Records and Statistics

YEAR	TICKER SYMBOL	DATE ADDED	CLOSING PRICE	BUY DATE	OPENING PRICE	TARGET PRICE	STOP PRICE	HIGH PRICE	DATE	W/L	DAYS	P/L
2008	XRAY	11/13/2008	$29.99	2/5/2009	$25.50	$28.05	$20.40	$28.36	4/29/2009	W	58	10%
2008	BUCY	11/13/2008	$25.00	2/5/2009	$15.21	$16.73	$12.17	$18.11	2/6/2009	W	2	10%
2008	ME	11/14/2008	$12.50	2/6/2009	$11.40	$12.54	$9.12	S.O	2/24/2009	L	12	-20%
2008	BIO	11/21/2008	$69.95	2/13/2009	$65.82	$72.40	$52.66	S.O	2/27/2009	L	10	-20%
2008	HITT	11/21/2008	$26.80	2/13/2009	$26.26	$28.89	$21.01	$29.08	3/6/2009	W	15	10%
2008	GEO	11/21/2008	$17.18	2/13/2009	$13.81	$15.19	$11.05	S.O	2/23/2009	L	6	-20%
2008	AXYS	11/21/2008	$61.83	2/13/2009	$39.46	$43.41	$31.57	S.O	3/2/2009	L	11	-20%
2008	WCN	12/1/2008	$26.71	2/23/2009	$25.53	$28.08	$20.42	C.O	5/18/2009	L	60	-1%
2008	STBA	12/1/2008	$32.71	2/23/2009	$23.46	$25.81	$18.77	S.O	3/5/2009	L	9	-20%
2008	MTD	12/1/2008	$76.30	2/23/2009	$55.20	$60.72	$44.16	S.O	3/13/2009	L	15	-20%
2008	TMP	12/1/2008	$53.00	2/23/2009	$41.87	$46.06	$33.50	S.O	3/5/2009	L	9	-20%
2008	DNB	12/1/2008	$78.00	2/23/2009	$74.49	$81.94	$59.59	$82.83	4/29/2009	W	47	10%
2008	THOR	12/1/2008	$23.88	2/23/2009	$24.49	$26.94	$19.59	$27.15	4/3/2009	W	30	10%
2008	FCN	12/4/2008	$53.15	2/26/2009	$38.22	$42.04	$30.58	$42.36	3/2/2009	W	3	10%
2008	MASI	12/18/2008	$28.10	3/12/2009	$26.05	$28.66	$20.84	$29.23	3/26/2009	W	11	10%
2008	EQT	12/18/2008	$31.64	3/12/2009	$29.95	$32.95	$23.96	$33.73	3/18/2009	W	5	10%
2008	WGOV	12/18/2008	$21.73	3/12/2009	$9.91	$10.90	$7.93	$12.43	3/26/2009	W	11	10%
2008	FORR	12/18/2008	$24.81	3/12/2009	$17.65	$19.42	$14.12	$19.99	3/18/2009	W	5	10%
2008	SLG	12/22/2008	$26.16	3/16/2009	$12.42	$13.66	$9.94	$13.89	3/19/2009	W	4	10%
2008	OHI	12/31/2008	$15.97	3/24/2009	$14.62	$16.08	$11.70	$16.49	4/24/2009	W	23	10%
2008	OI	12/31/2008	$27.33	3/24/2009	$13.41	$14.75	$10.73	$15.05	3/25/2009	W	2	10%
2008	FLIR	12/31/2008	$30.68	3/24/2009	$21.06	$23.17	$16.85	$23.37	4/27/2009	W	24	10%
2008	VLY	12/31/2008	$20.25	3/24/2009	$12.04	$13.24	$9.63	$13.44	4/2/2009	W	8	10%
2008	AMSF	12/31/2008	$20.53	3/24/2009	$15.53	$17.08	$12.42	$17.58	4/9/2009	W	13	10%
2008	ATU	12/31/2008	$19.02	3/24/2009	$8.65	$9.52	$6.92	$9.75	3/25/2009	W	2	10%
2008	INDB	12/31/2008	$26.16	3/24/2009	$16.75	$18.43	$13.40	$19.75	4/13/2009	W	14	10%
2008	FSP	12/31/2008	$14.75	3/24/2009	$12.76	$14.04	$10.21	$14.27	4/9/2009	W	13	10%

Recommended Resources:

The Trading Pro System -This course contains over 24 hours of teaching by Dave, in which he covers the options strategies and other techniques that he uses in the daily reviews on this site. These are the techniques that really make money from the market!

For more information on The Trading Pro System visit our website at: http://www.beyondoptionstrading.com

Daily Market Advantage - The daily market reviews are very helpful to make sure you're on the right track and making the best trades each day. When you sign up using this exclusive bonus offer, you will receive a30 day trial of the Daily Market Advantage for only $9.95

For more information on The Daily Market Advantage visit our website at: http://www.beyondoptionstrading.com/dma

---

Want A Digital Version Of This Book?

Get a digital PDF version of Tailwind Trading System and the companion book Penny Stock Castaways plus for a limited time you get two more great stock option trading e-books:
"IPO Secrets" and "Mergers and Acquisitions Profits"

Visit Our Website For More Details

http://www.beyondoptionstrading.com

www.ingramcontent.com/pod-product-compliance
Lightning Source LLC
Chambersburg PA
CBHW081128170526
45165CB00008B/2592